RECORDED VERSIONS GUITAR

AUTHENTIC TRANSCRIPTIONS
WITH NOTES AND TABLATURE

Django Reinhardt
THE DEFINITIVE COLLECTION

Cover photo courtesy of Frank Driggs Collection

Music transcriptions by Pete Billmann

ISBN 0-634-03430-8

HAL•LEONARD®
CORPORATION

7777 W. BLUEMOUND RD. P.O. BOX 13819 MILWAUKEE, WI 53213

Visit Hal Leonard Online at www.halleonard.com

CONTENTS

Ain't Misbehavin'

Words by Andy Razaf
Music by Thomas "Fats" Waller and Harry Brooks

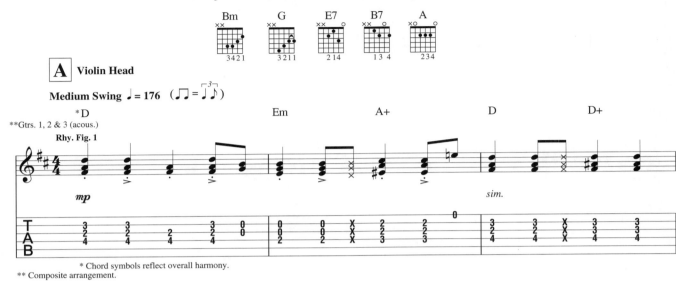

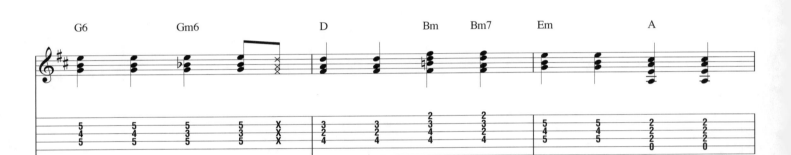

* Chord symbols reflect overall harmony.
** Composite arrangement.

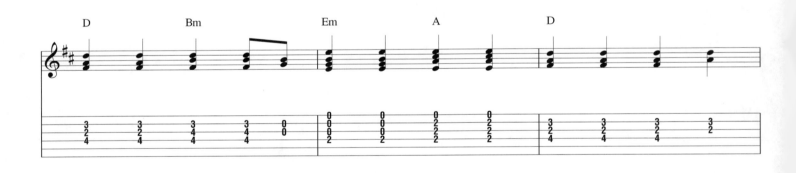

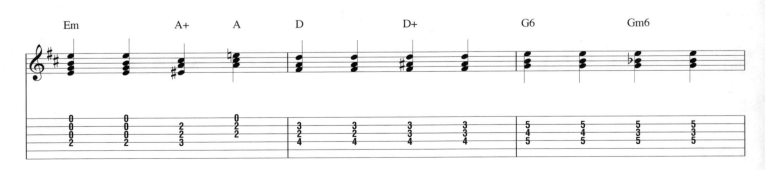

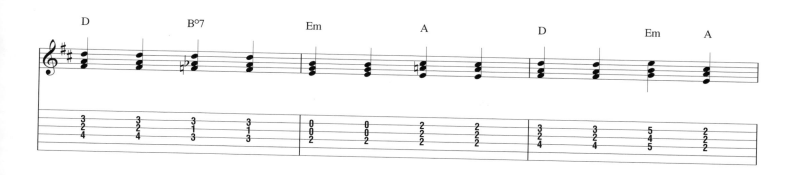

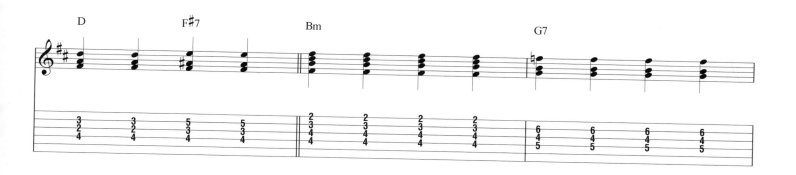

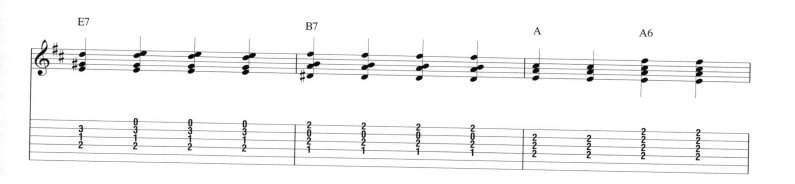

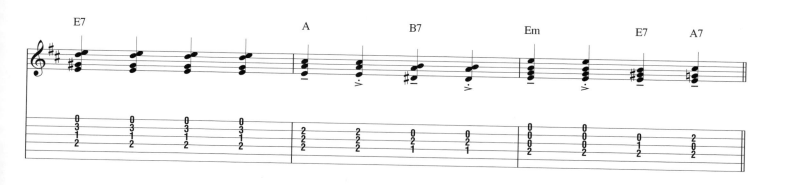

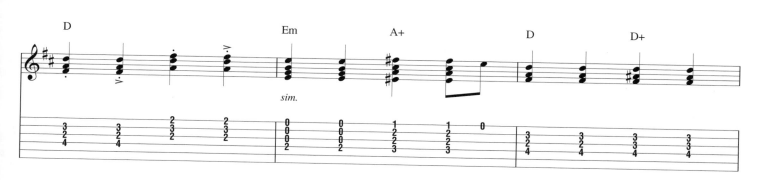

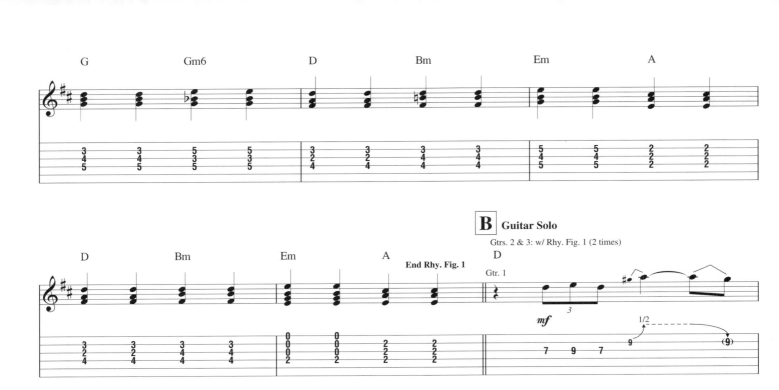

B **Guitar Solo**

Gtrs. 2 & 3: w/ Rhy. Fig. 1 (2 times)

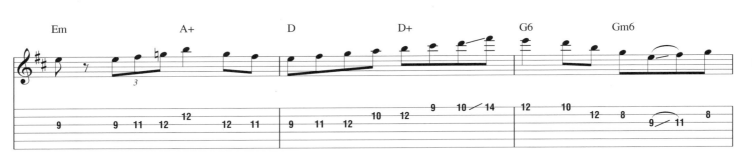

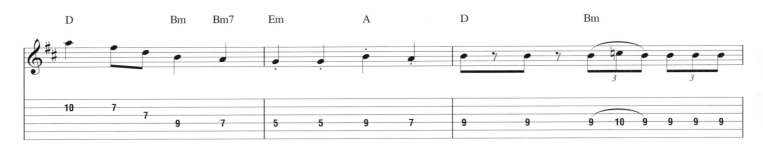

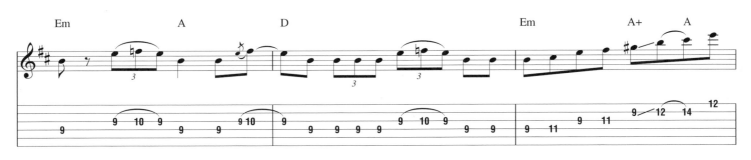

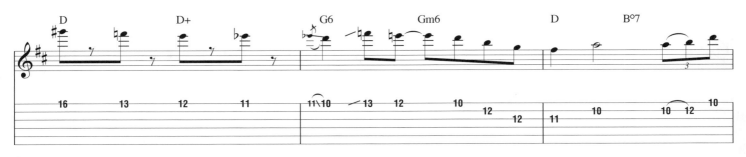

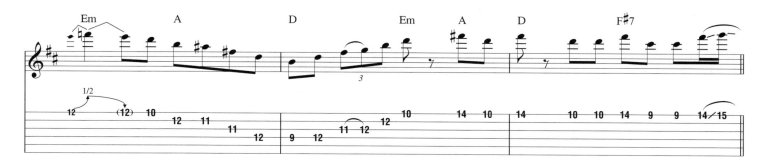

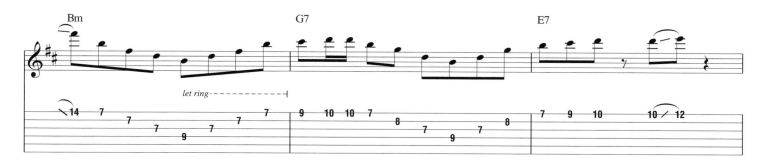

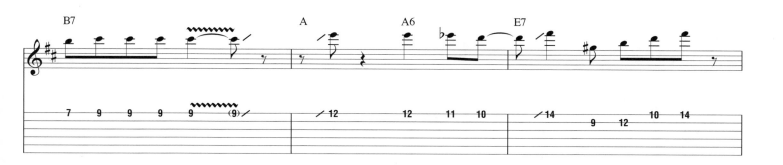

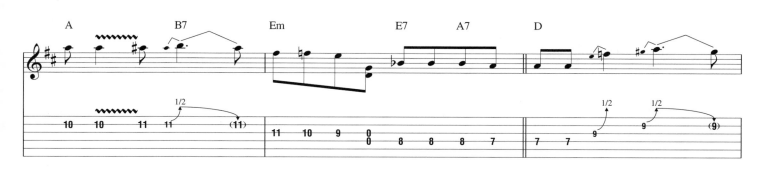

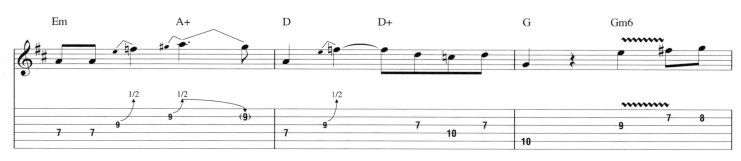

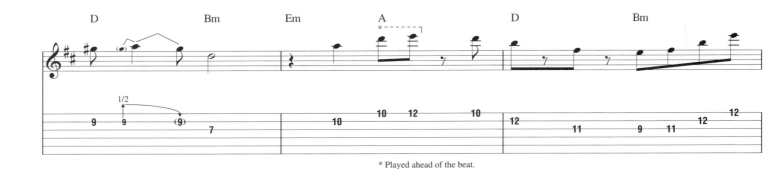

* Played ahead of the beat.

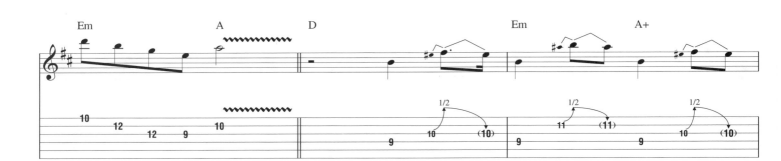

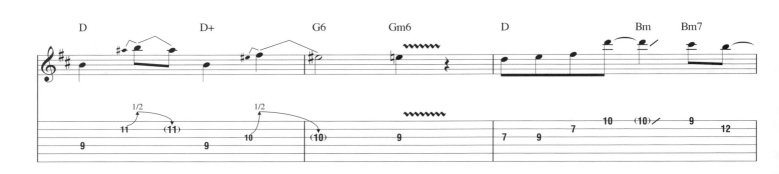

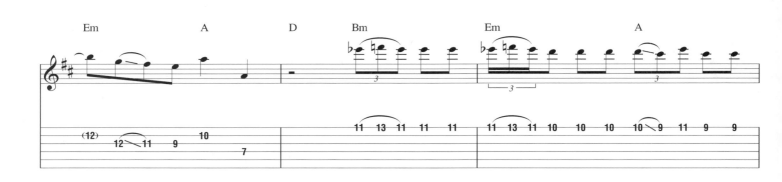

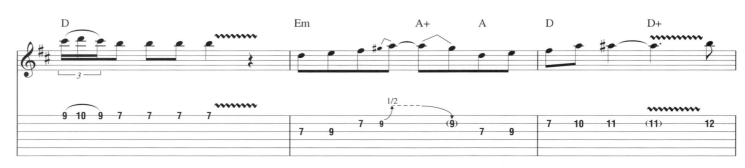

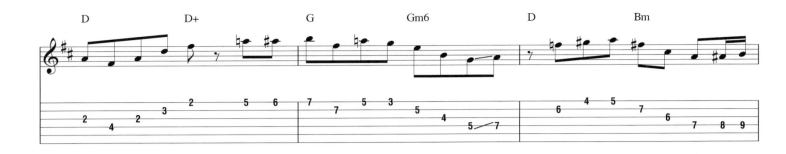

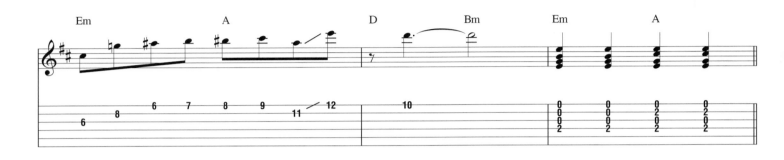

E

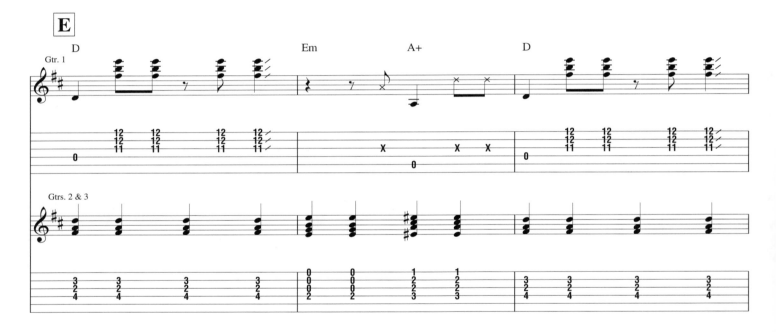

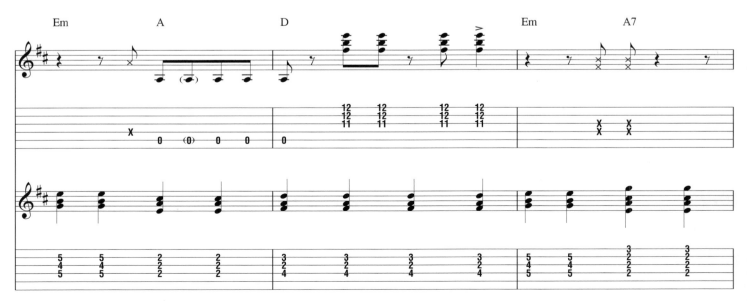

10

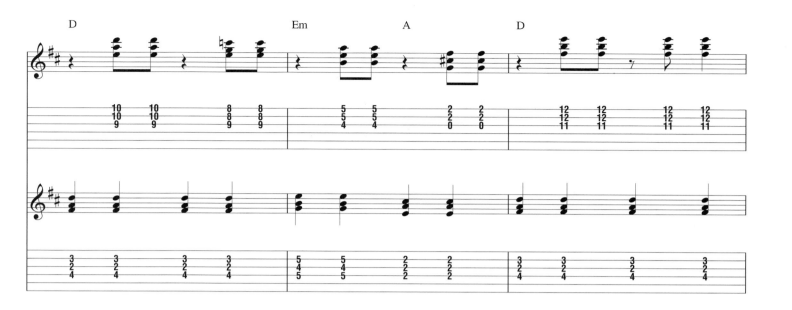

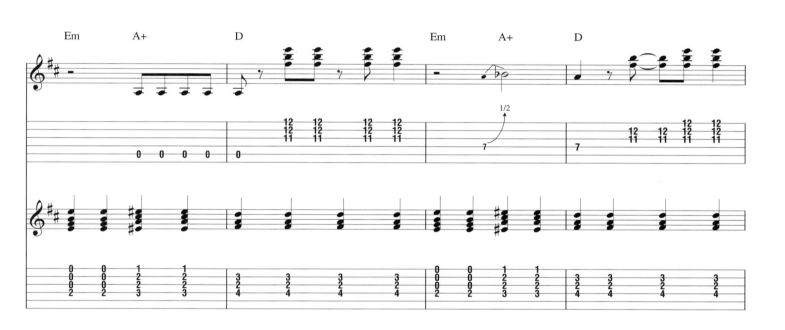

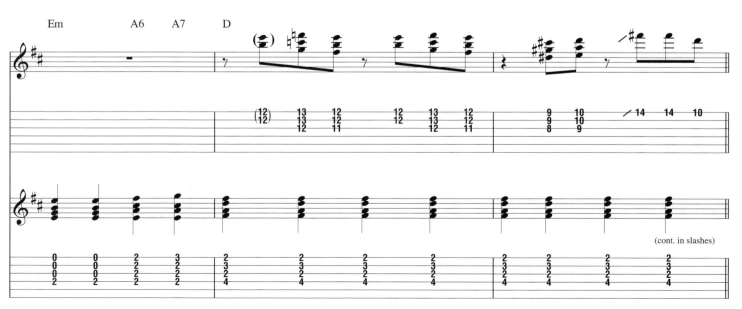

(cont. in slashes)

from *Djangology*

Belleville

By Django Reinhardt

A Intro

Moderately fast Swing ♩ = 220

*Gtr. 2

*Clarinet arr. for gtr.

Gtr. 1 (acous.)

**Played as even eighth notes.

Gtr. 3 (acous.)

A7

(cont. in slashes)

B Head

D   A7type2   D   A7type2

Gtr. 3

sim.

Gtr. 2

Gtr. 1

***T(5 & 6)   T(5 & 6)

***T(5 & 6) = Thumb on 5th and 6th strings.

*T(6) = Thumb on 6th string.

15

C Guitar Solo

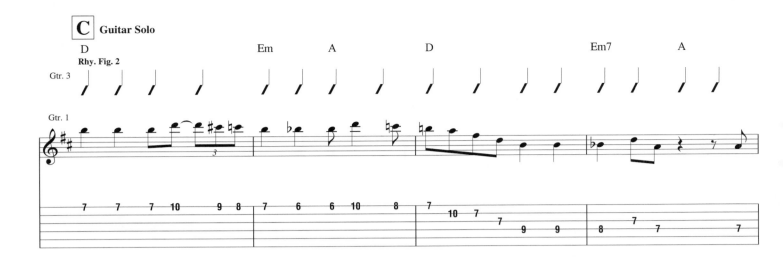

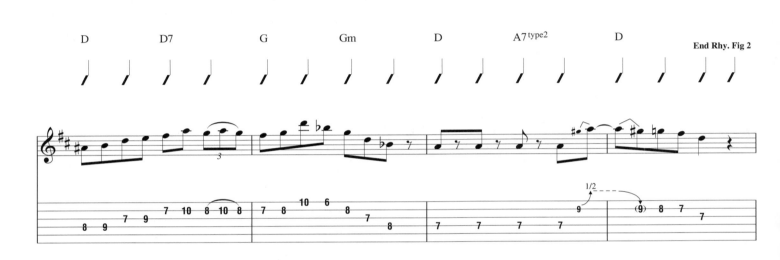

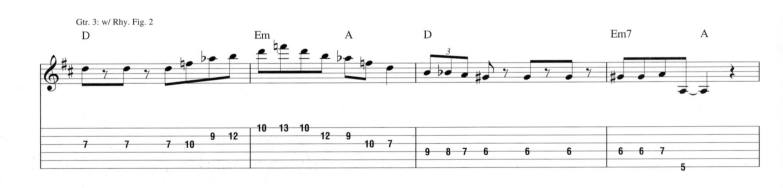

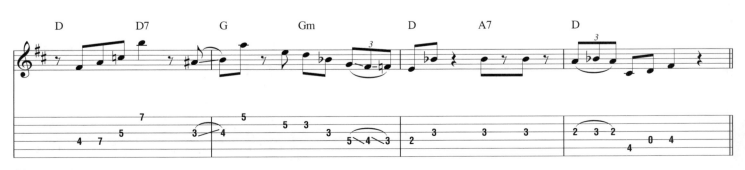

*Played as even eighth notes.

Daphne

By Django Reinhardt

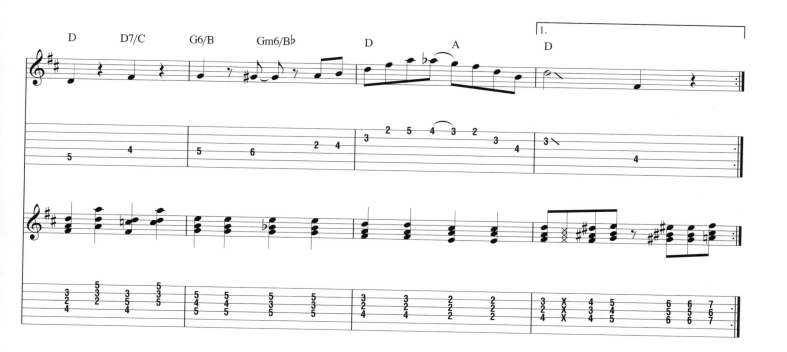

*Chord symbols reflect overall harmony.
***Composite arrangement.

**Violin arr. for gtr.

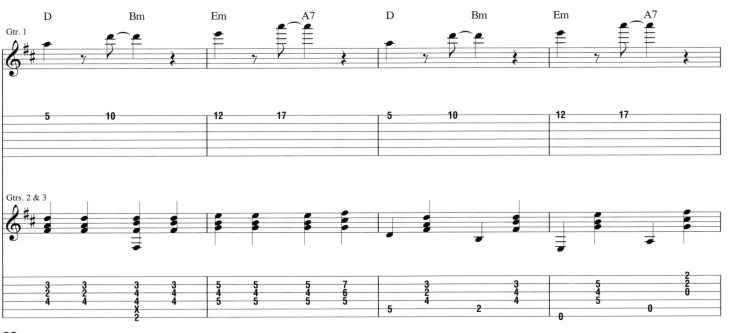

(cont. in slashes)

B **Guitar Solo**

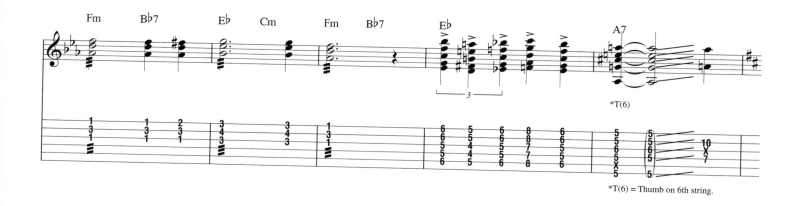

*T(6) = Thumb on 6th string.

Gtr. 3 tacet
Gtr. 2: w/ Rhy. Fig. 1 (1st 6 meas.)

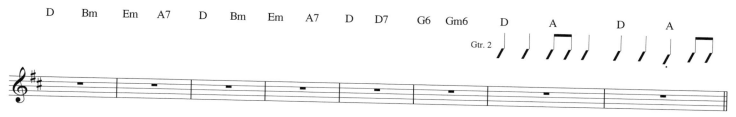

D Head

Gtr. 2: w/ Rhy. Fig. 1 (1 3/4 times)

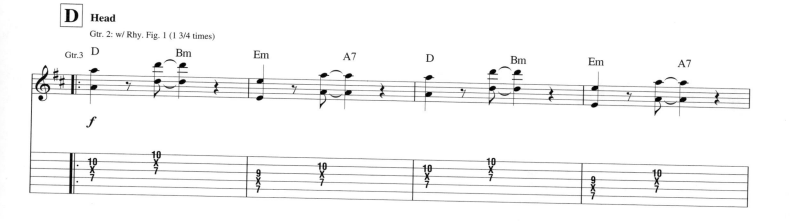

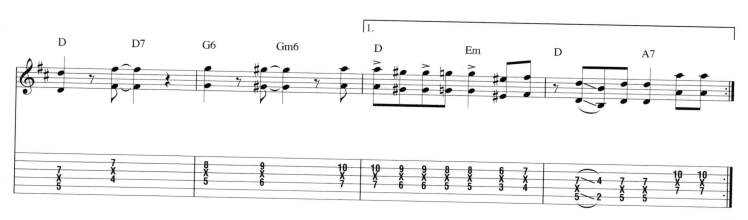

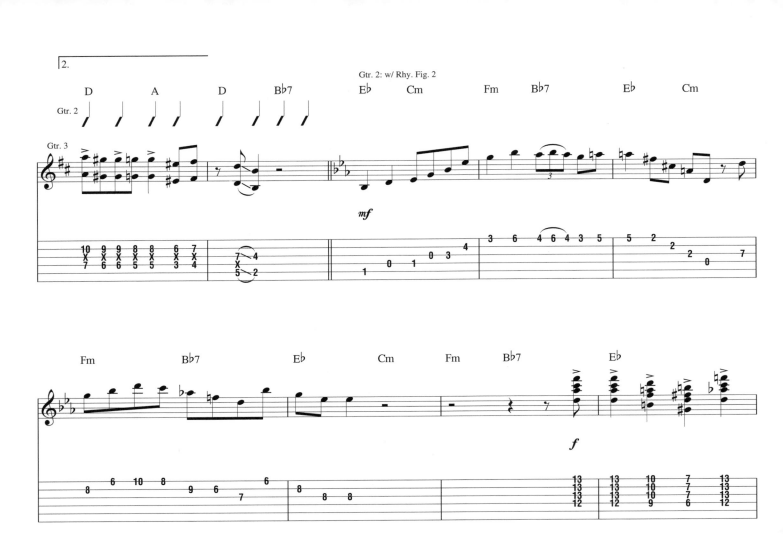

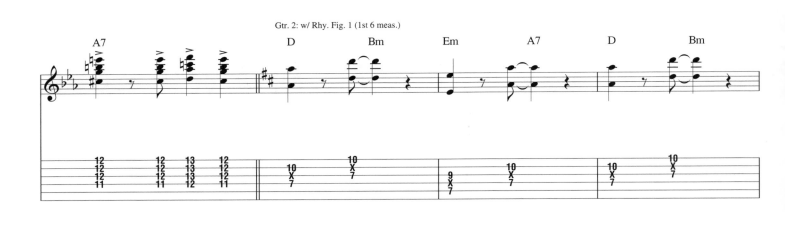

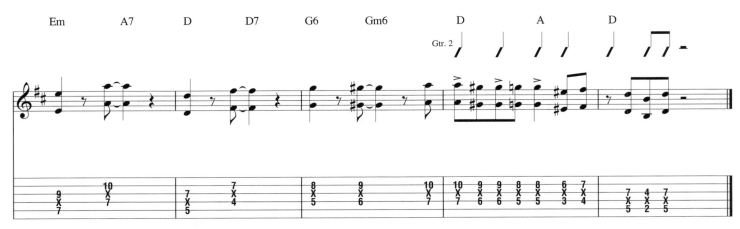

from *Djangology*

Dinah

Words by Sam M. Lewis and Joe Young
Music by Harry Akst

T(6) = Thumb on 6th string.

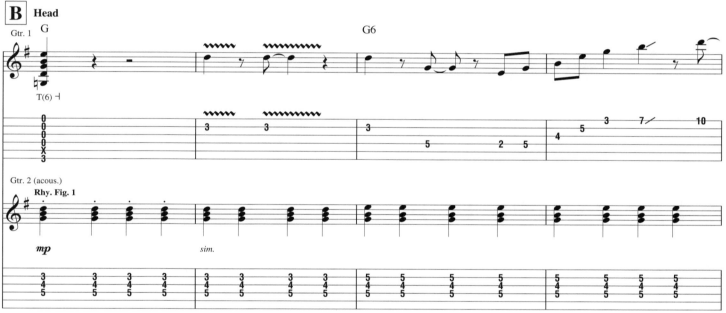

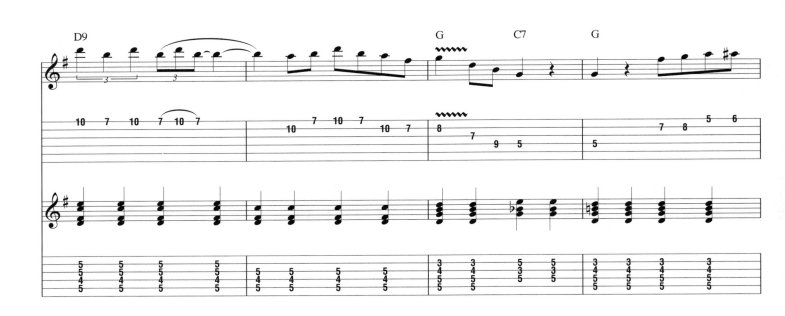

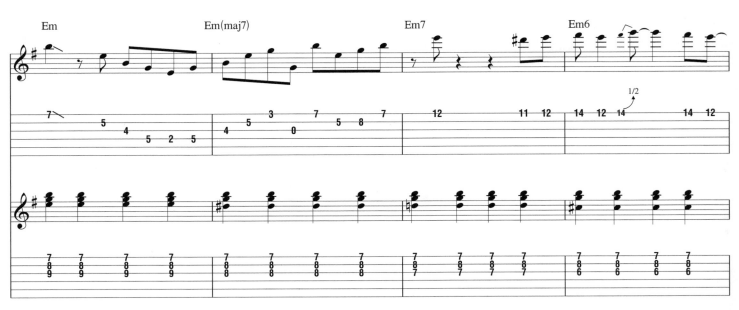

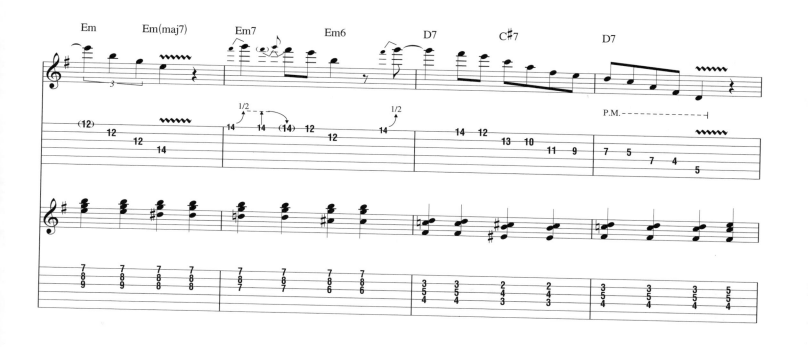

*Trill is picked rather than slurred.

End Rhy. Fig. 1

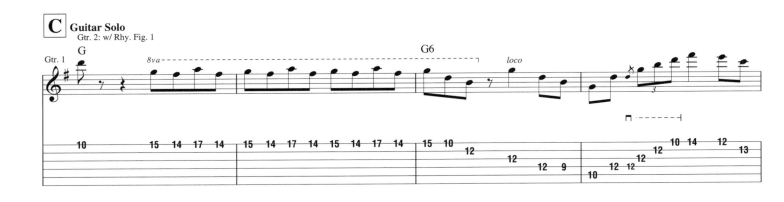

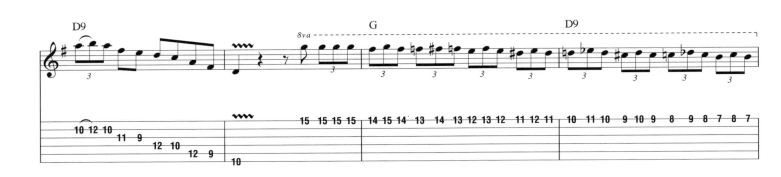

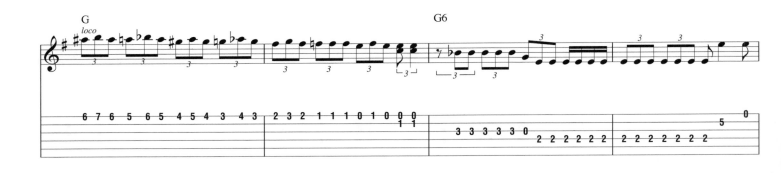

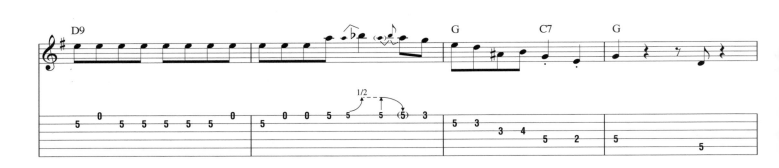

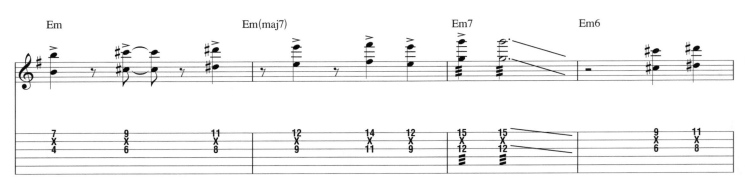

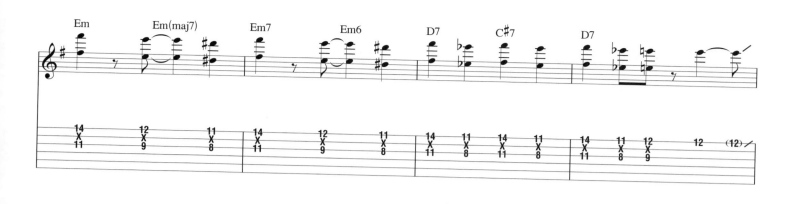

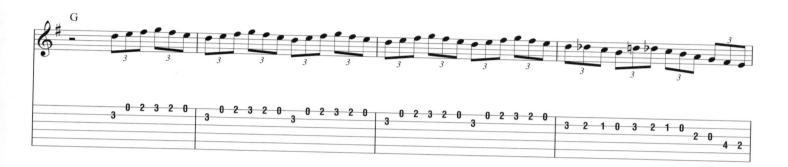

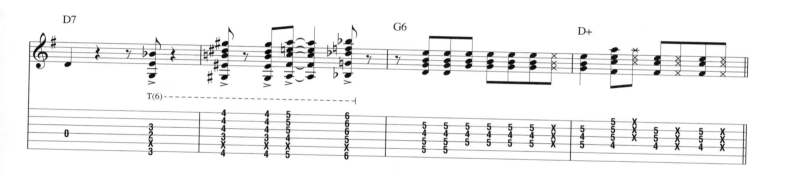

D **Violin Solo**

Gtr. 2: w/ Rhy. Fig. 1 (1 30/32 times)

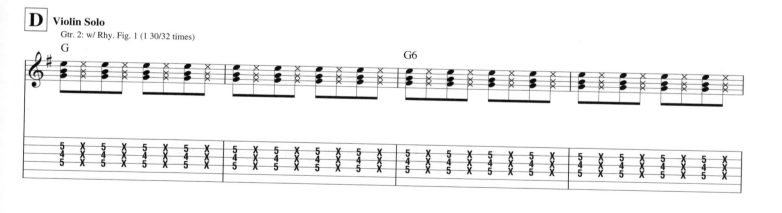

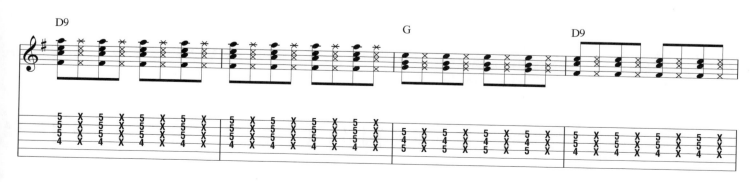

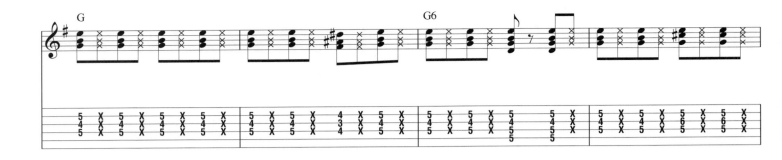

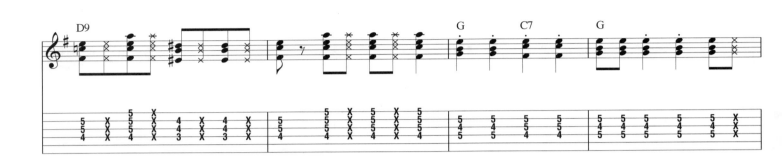

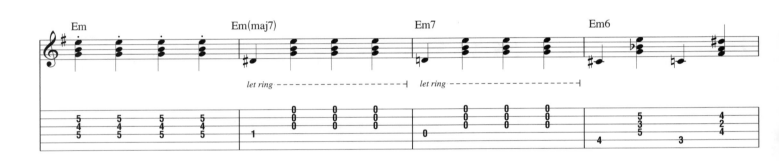

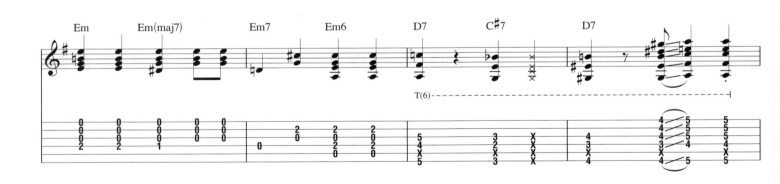

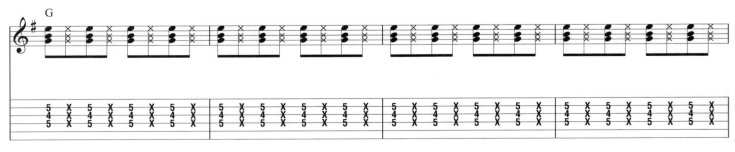

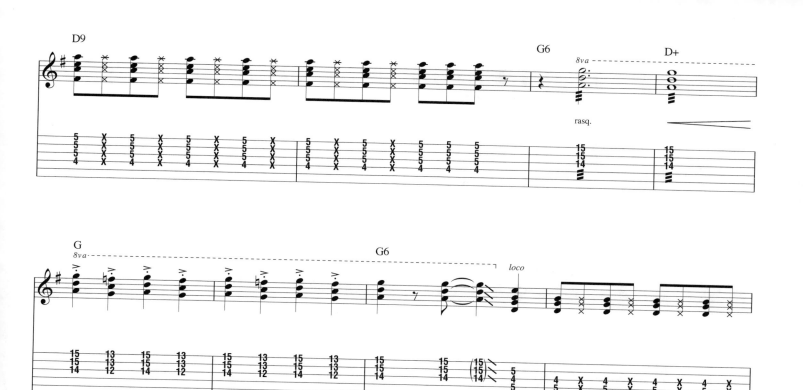

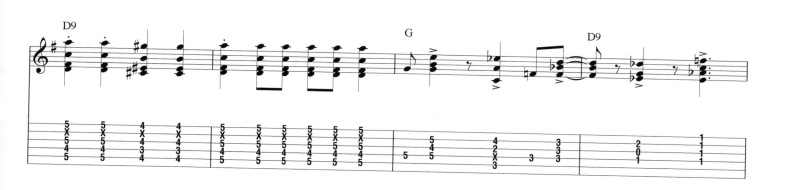

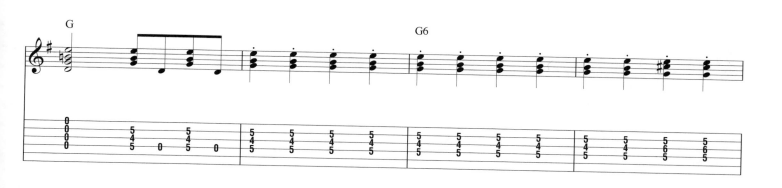

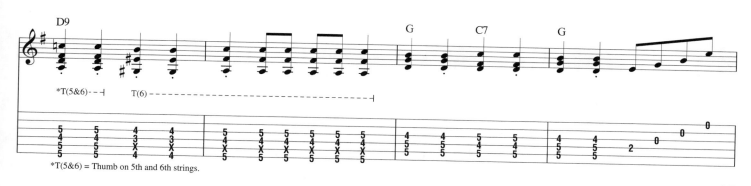

*T(5&6) = Thumb on 5th and 6th strings.

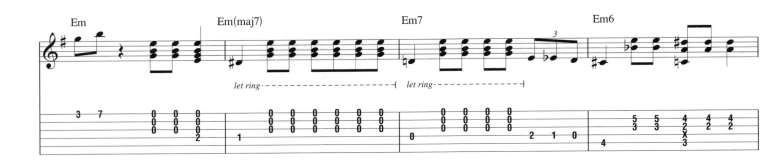

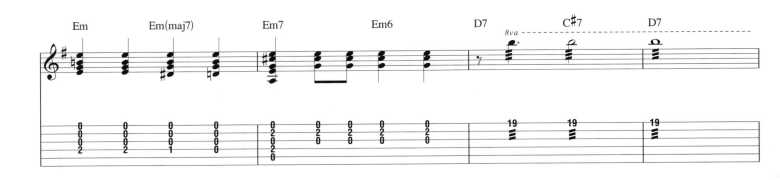

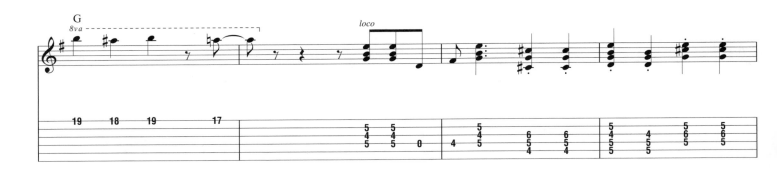

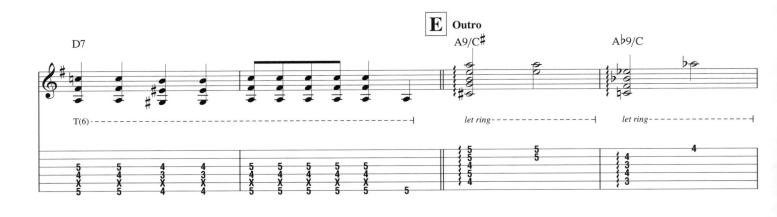

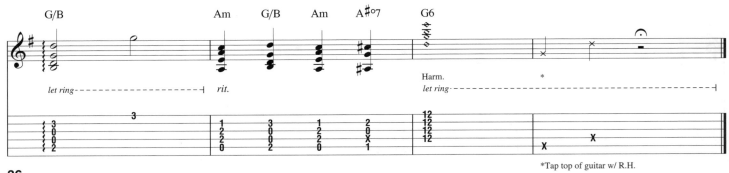

*Tap top of guitar w/ R.H.

from *Djangology*
Dinette
By Django Reinhardt

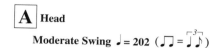

Moderate Swing ♩ = 202

** Clarinet arr. for gtr.

* Chord symbols reflect overall harmony.

*** T(5&6) = Thumb on 5th and 6th strings.

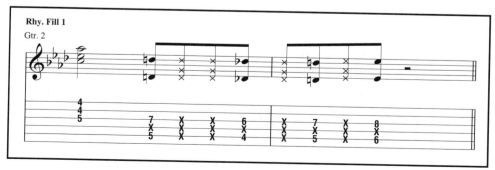

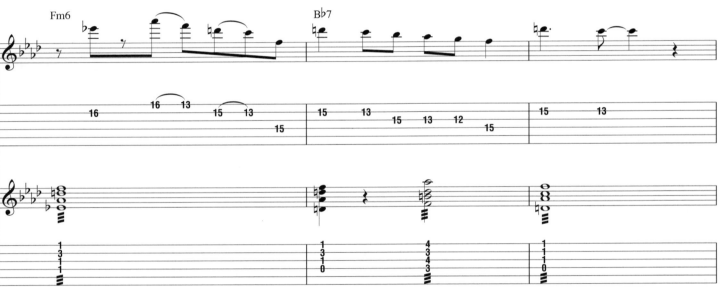

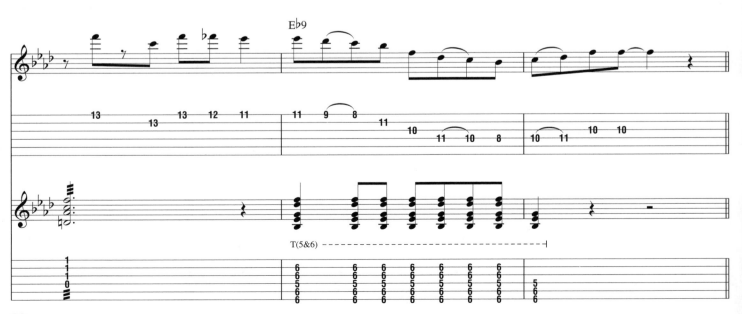

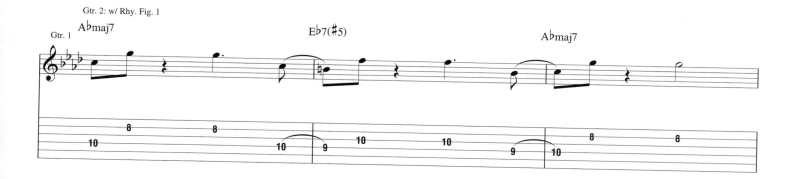

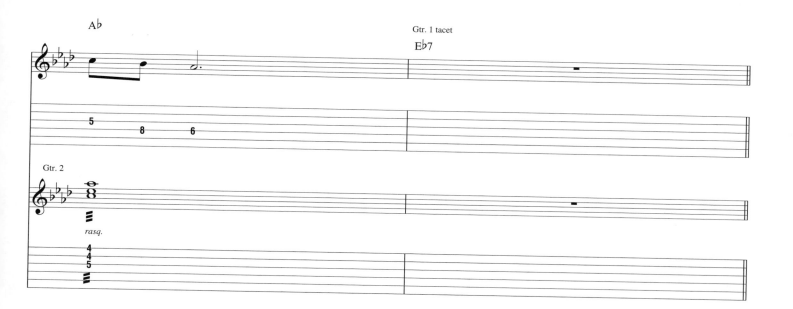

B **Guitar Solo**

* T(6) = Thumb on 6th string. (4th & 5th strings fretted with middle finger simultaneously.)

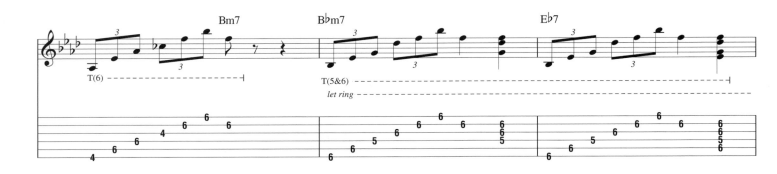

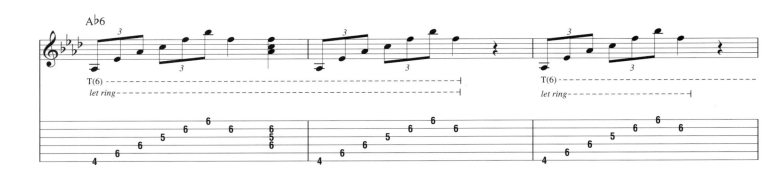

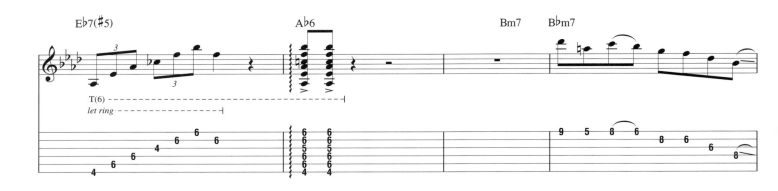

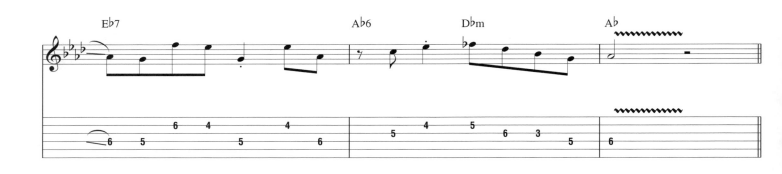

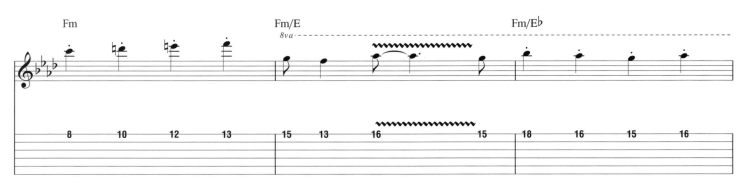

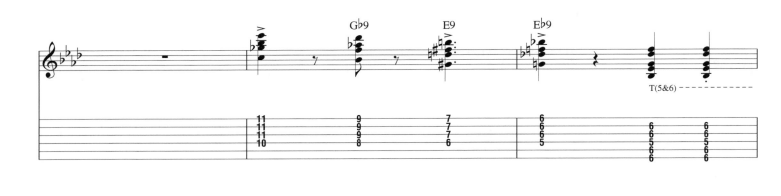

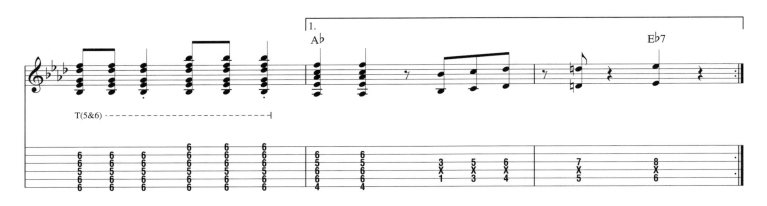

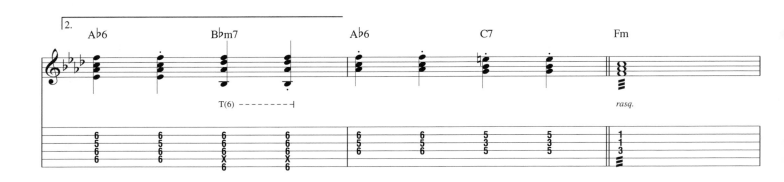

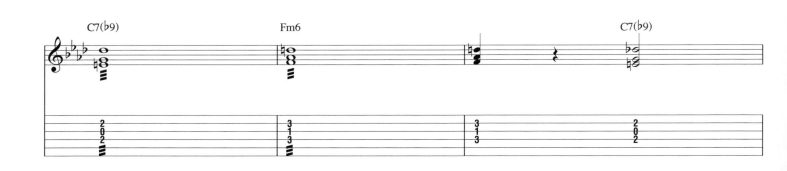

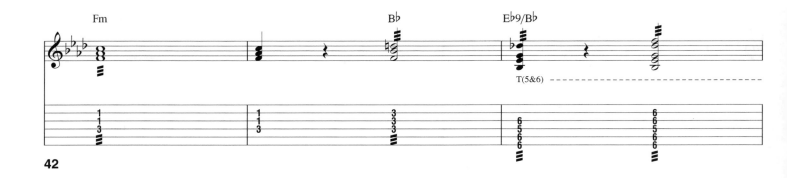

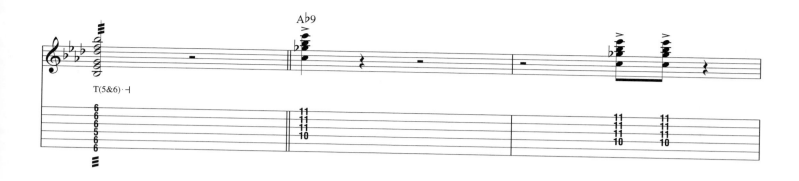

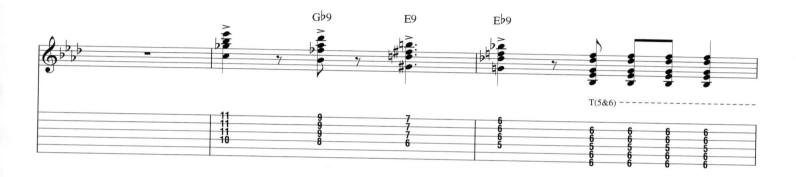

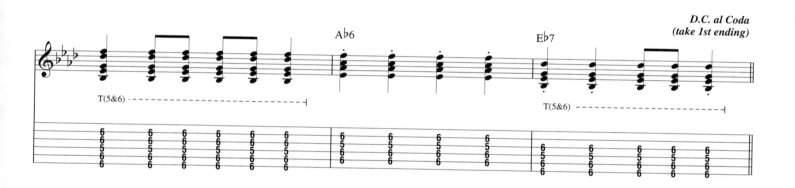

Coda

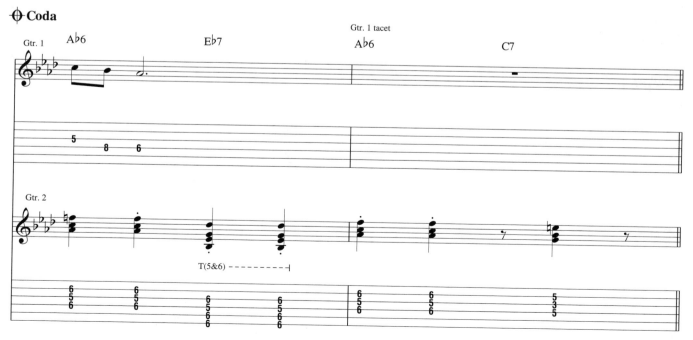

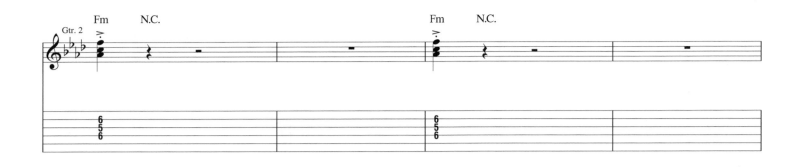

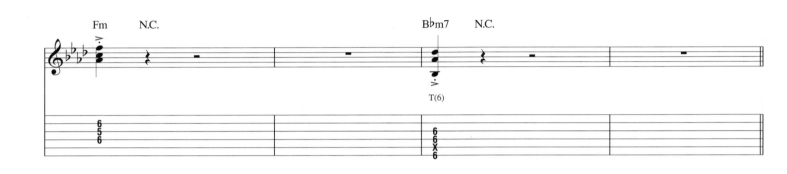

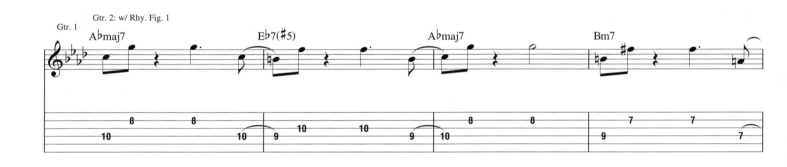

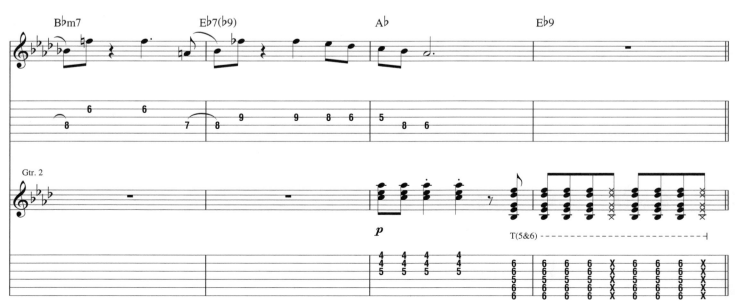

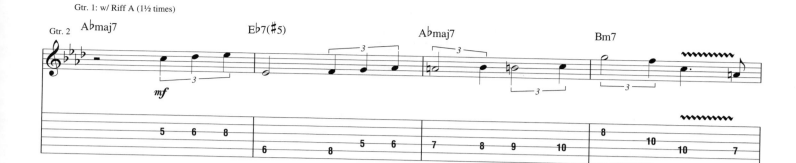

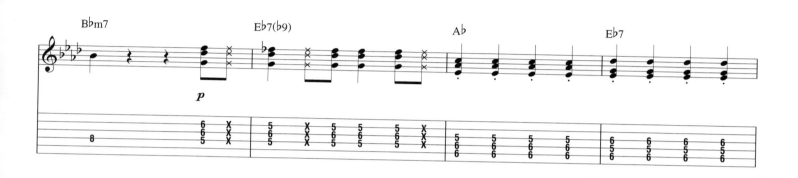

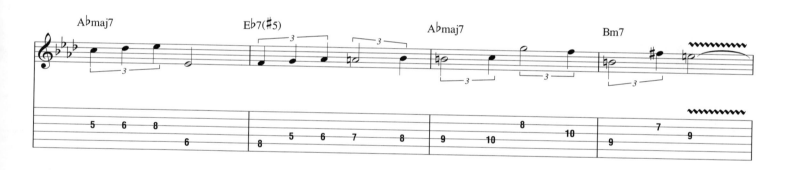

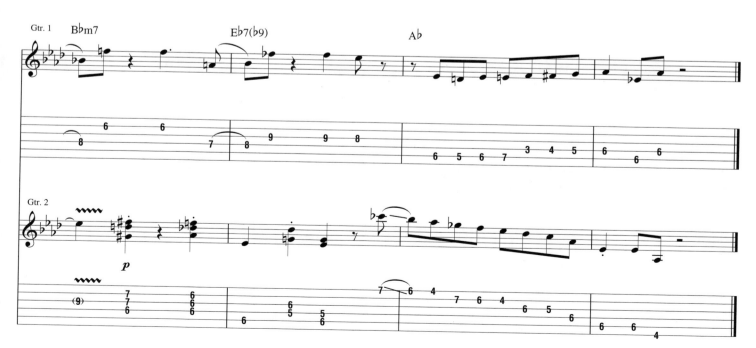

from *Djangology*

Djangology

By Django Reinhardt and Stephane Grappelli

A Intro

Moderately ♩ = 150

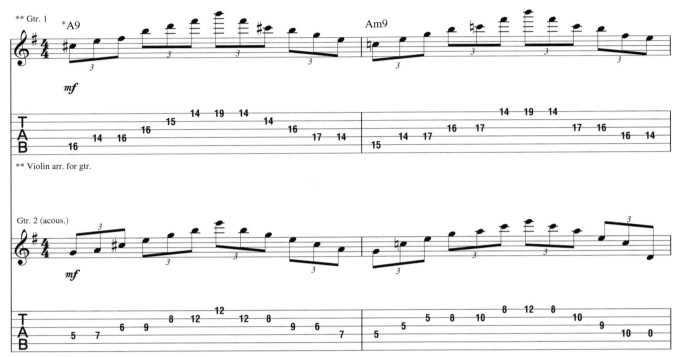

* Chord symbols reflect overall harmony.

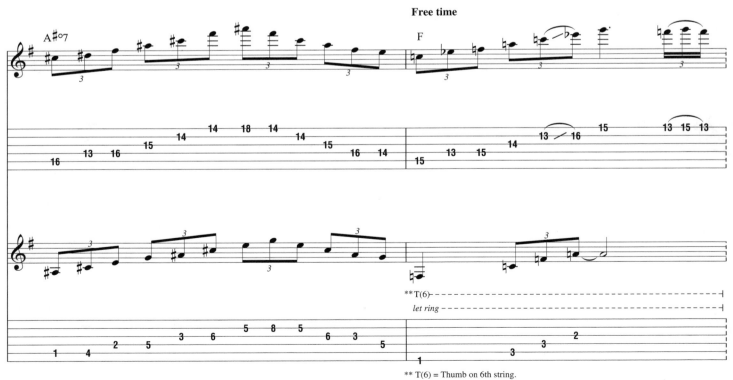

** T(6) = Thumb on 6th string.

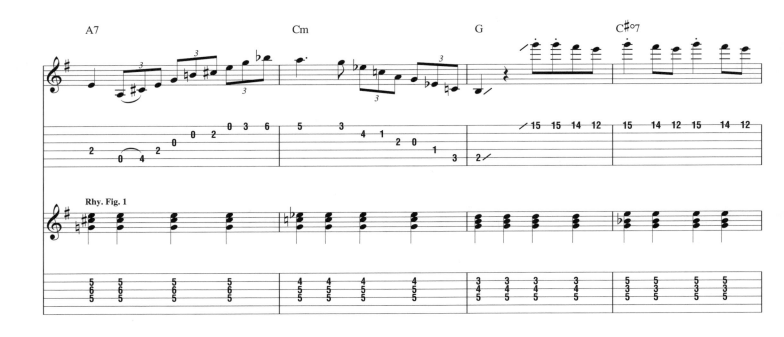

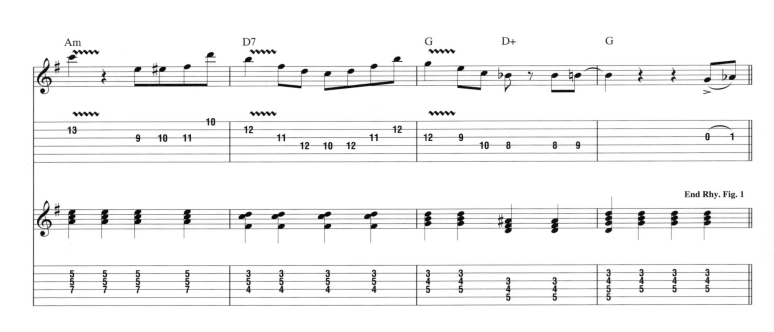

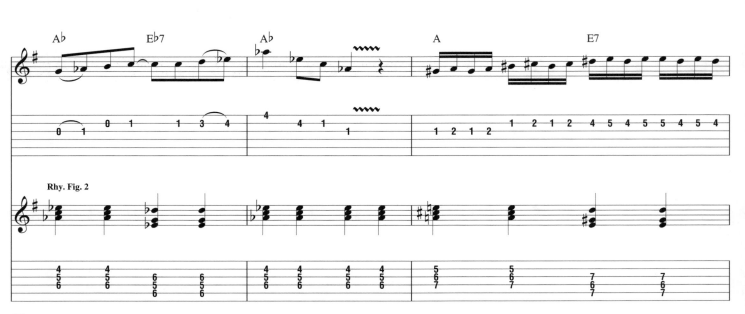

49

C Guitar Solo

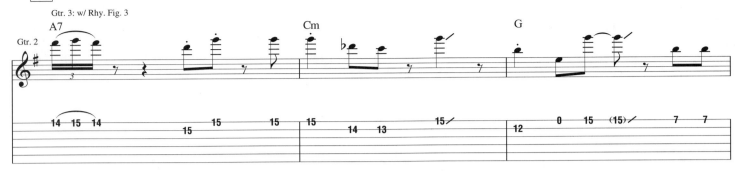

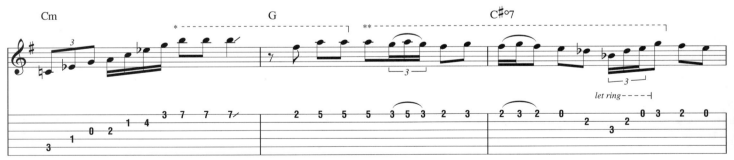

* Played as even eighth notes.　　** Played behind the beat.

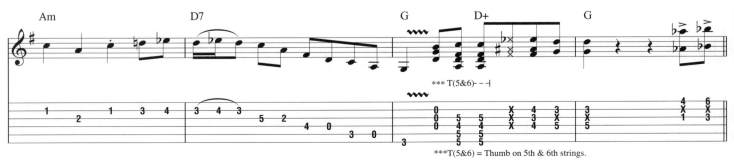

*** T(5&6) = Thumb on 5th & 6th strings.

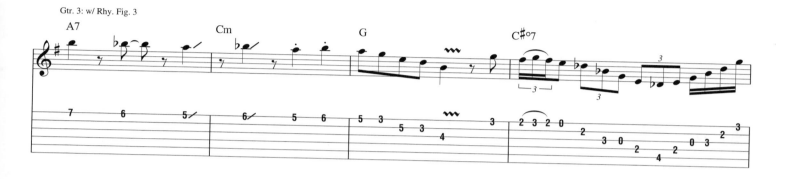

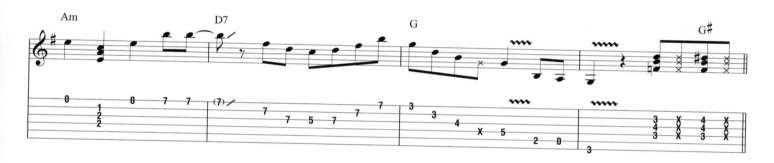

D **Violin Solo**

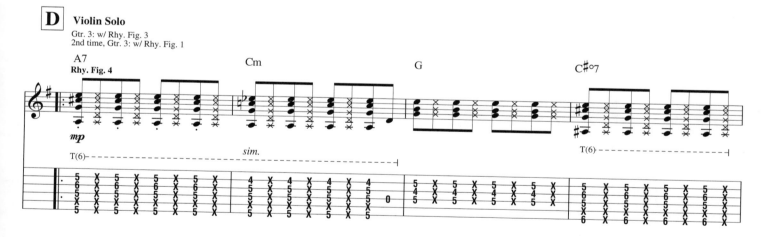

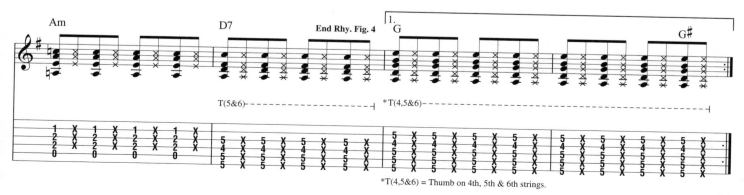

*T(4,5&6) = Thumb on 4th, 5th & 6th strings.

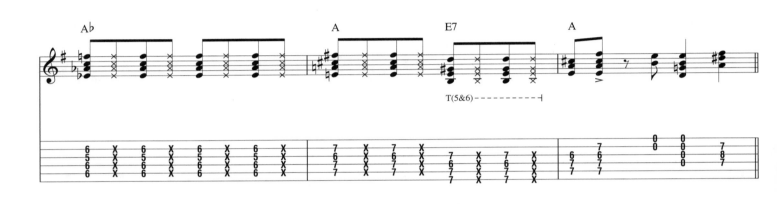

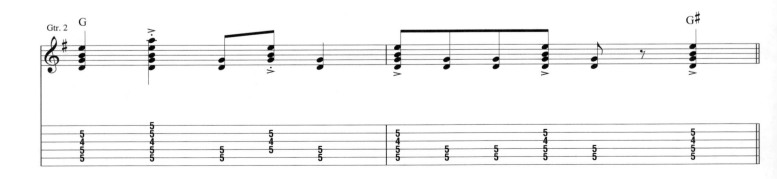

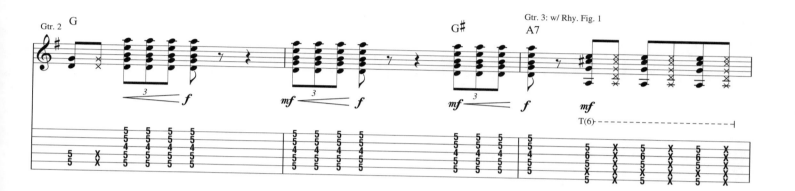

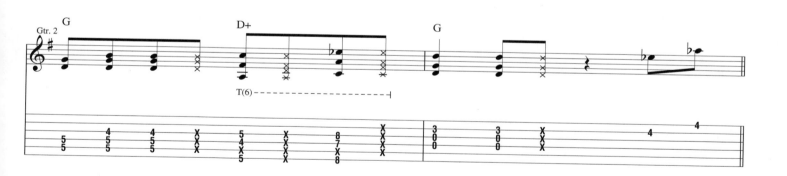

Gtr. 3: w/ Rhy. Fig. 3 (1st 6 meas.)

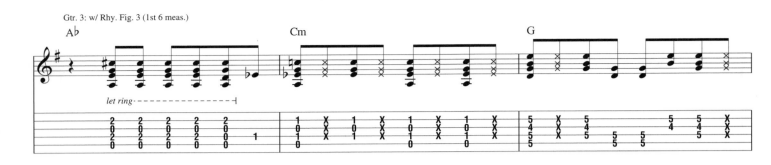

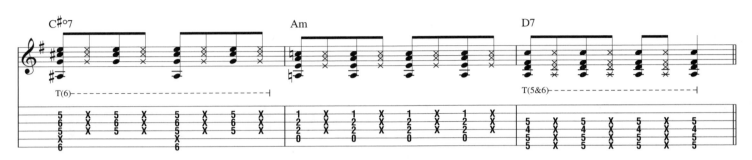

E Outro

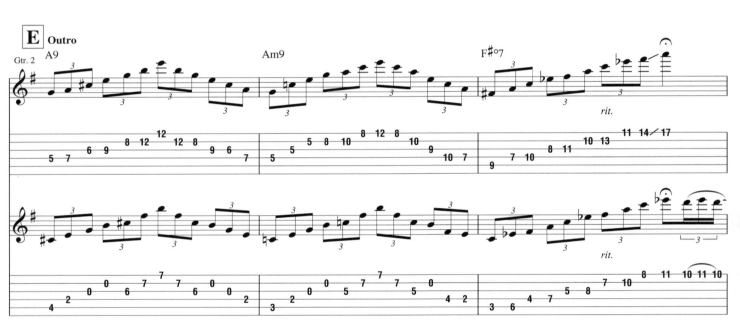

Free time

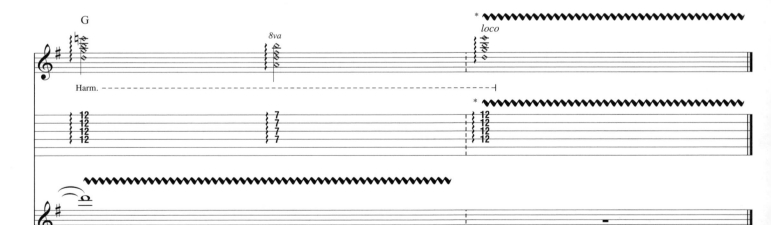

* Large vibrato produced by shaking guitar with large movements.

from *Swing Guitar*

Honeysuckle Rose

Words by Andy Razaf
Music by Thomas "Fats" Waller

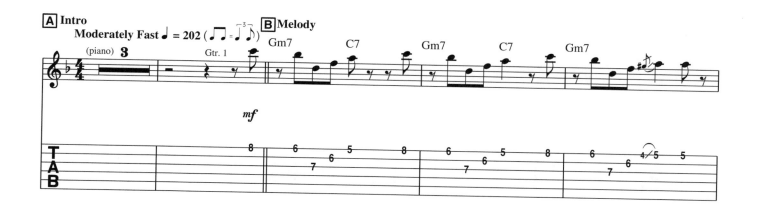

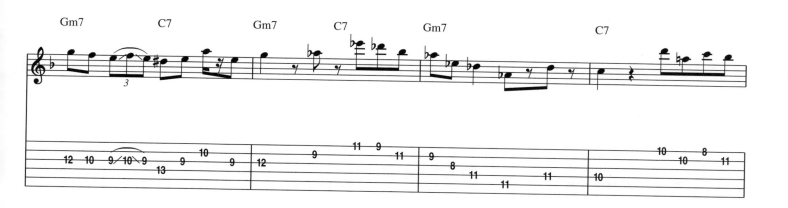

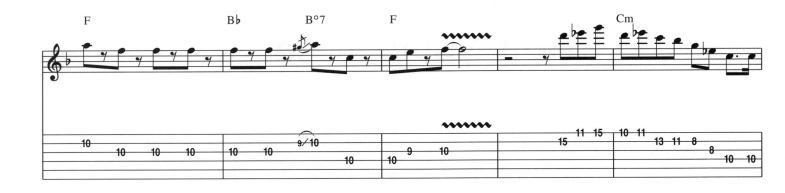

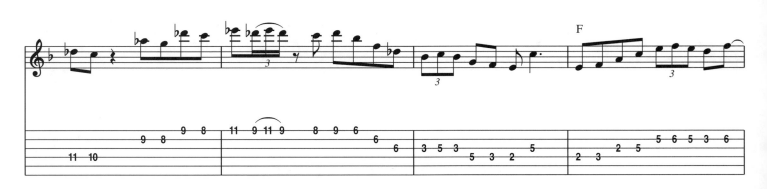

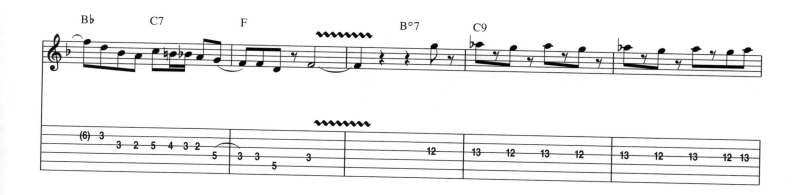

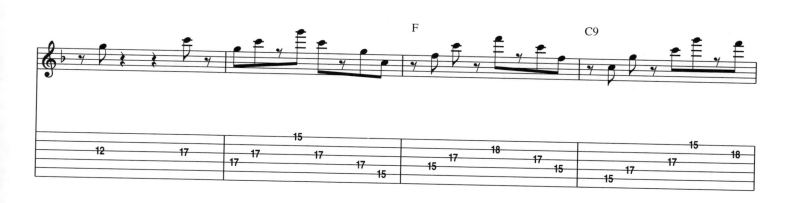

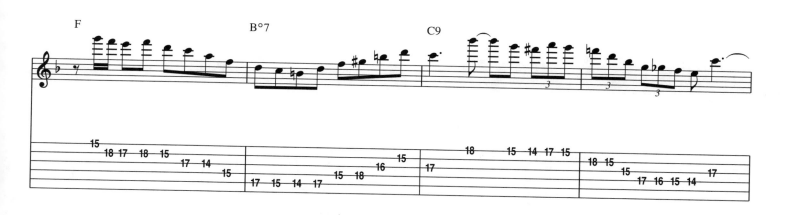

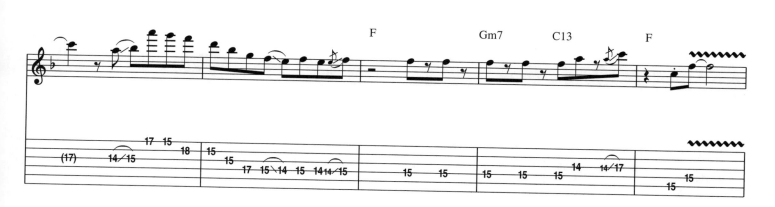

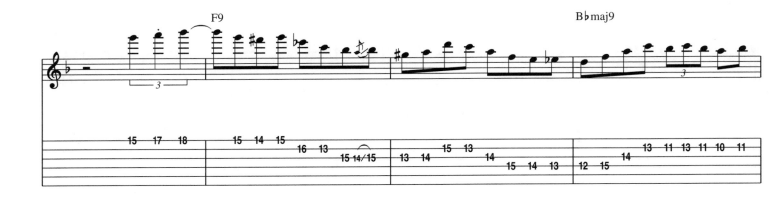

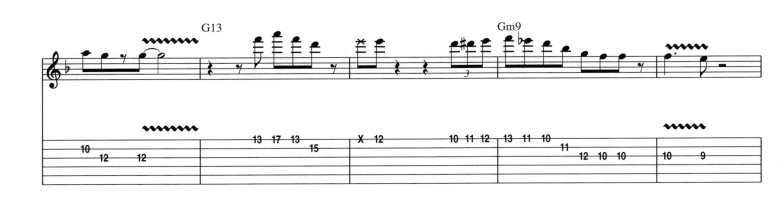

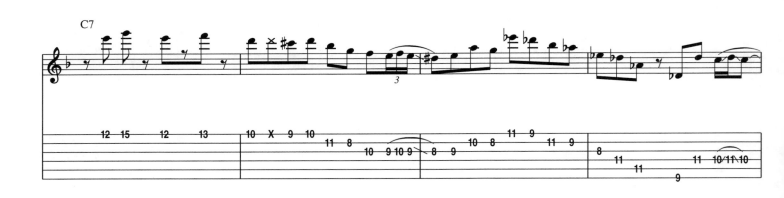

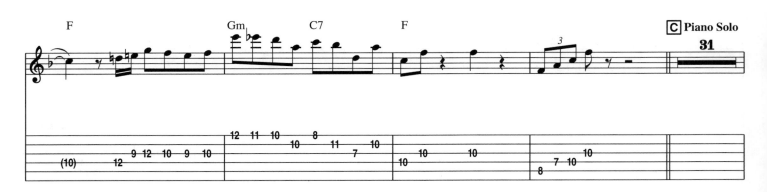

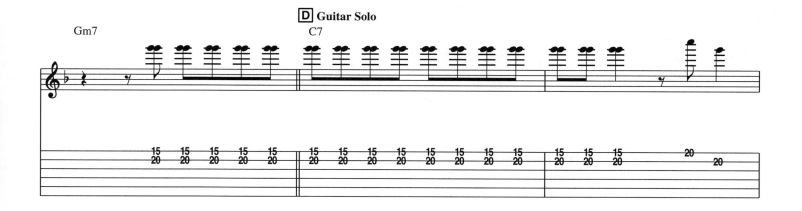

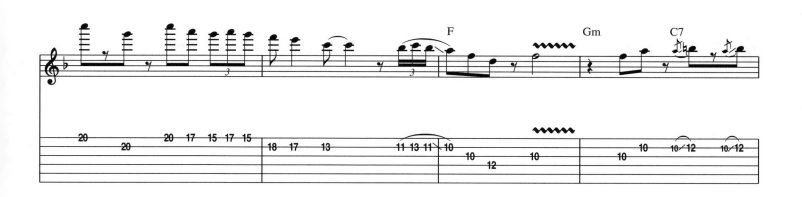

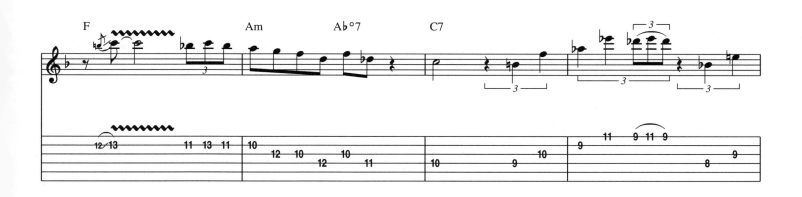

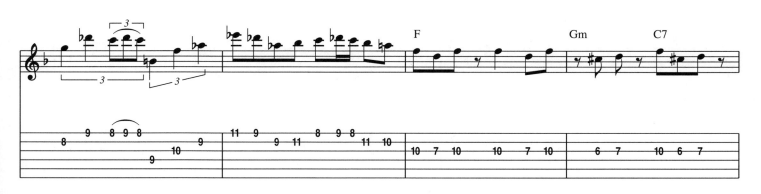

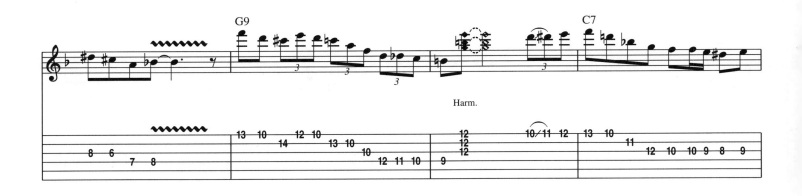

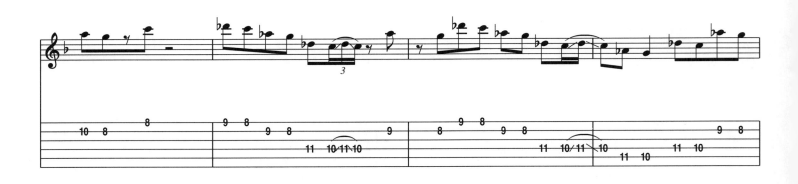

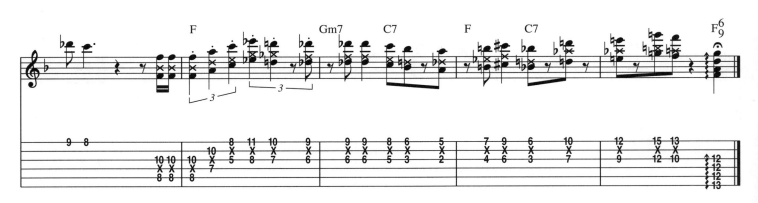

from *Djangology*

Limehouse Blues

Words by Douglas Furber
Music by Philip Braham

  Head

Fast Swing ♩ = 138

*C9

**Gtr. 1

mf

**Violin arr. for gtr.

***Gtr. 2 & 3 (acous.)

Rhy. Fig. 1

mf   *sim.*   *let ring - - - - - - -*

*** Composite arrangement.

* Chord symbols reflect overall harmony.

A7

End Rhy. Fig. 1

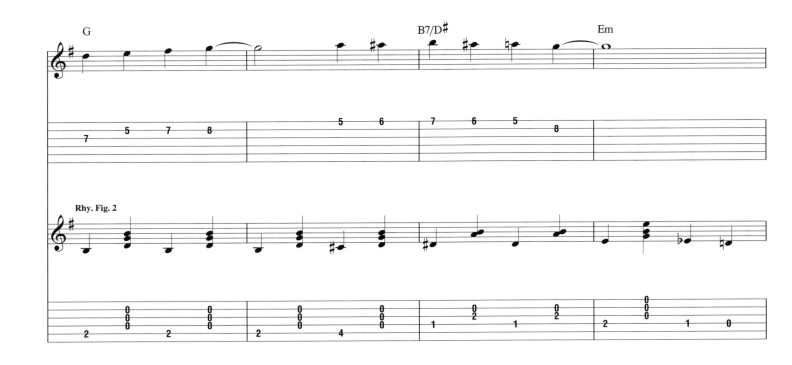

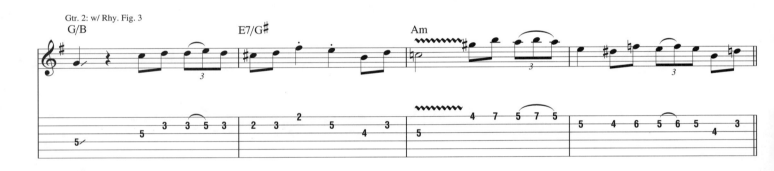

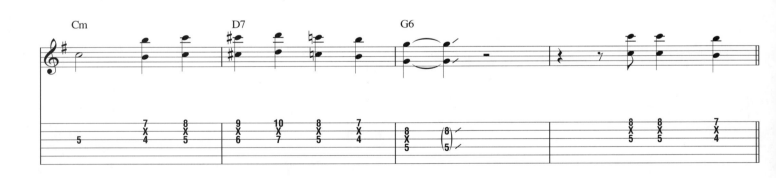

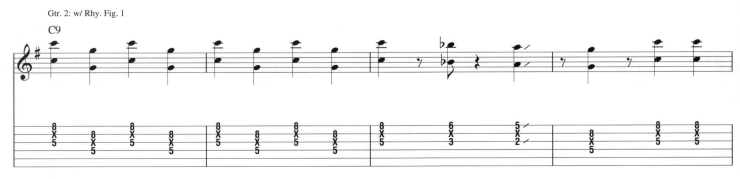

Gtr. 2: w/ Rhy. Fig. 2

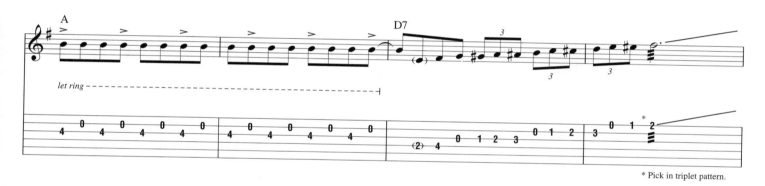

* Pick in triplet pattern.

Gtr. 2: w/ Rhy. Fig. 1

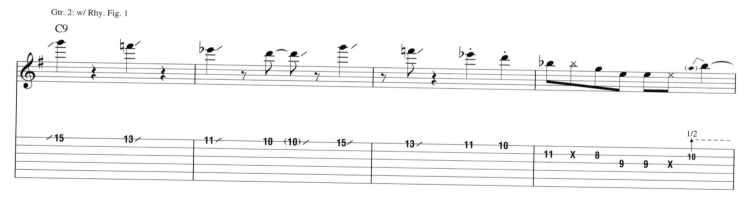

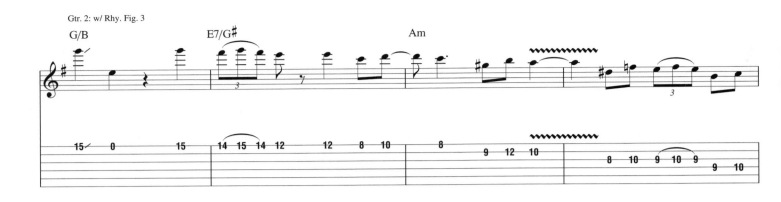

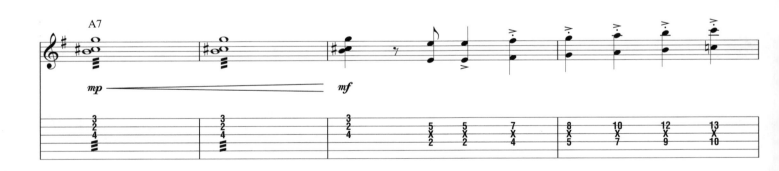

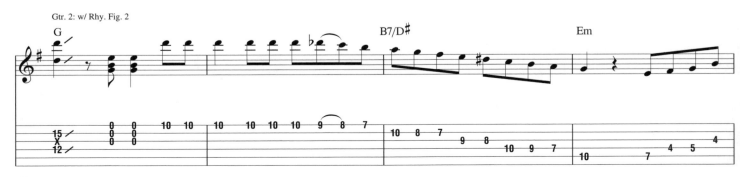

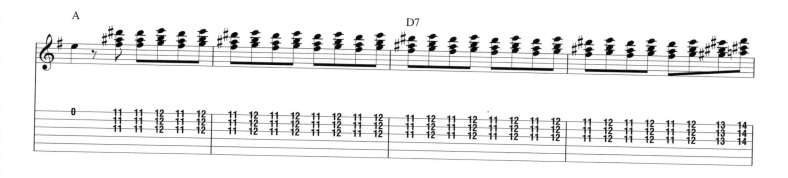

Gtr. 2: w/ Rhy. Fig. 1

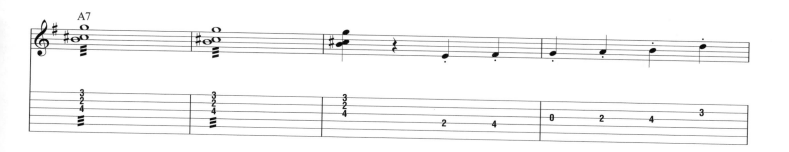

Gtr. 2: w/ Rhy. Fig. 3

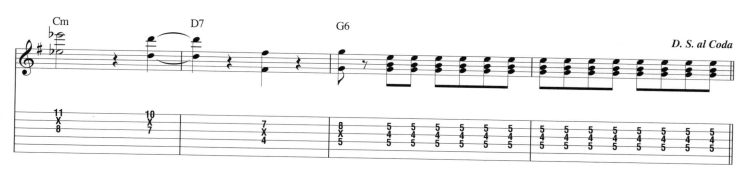

⊕ Coda

D Outro

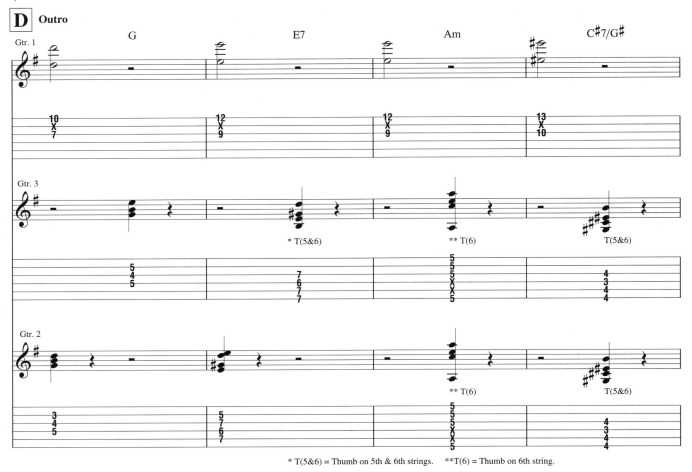

*T(5&6) = Thumb on 5th & 6th strings.   **T(6) = Thumb on 6th string.

Marie
Words and Music by Irving Berlin

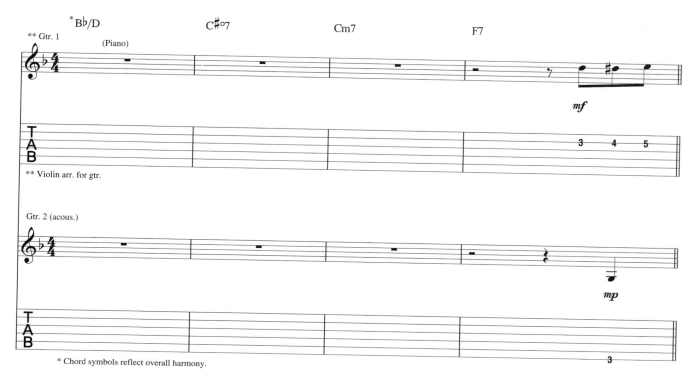

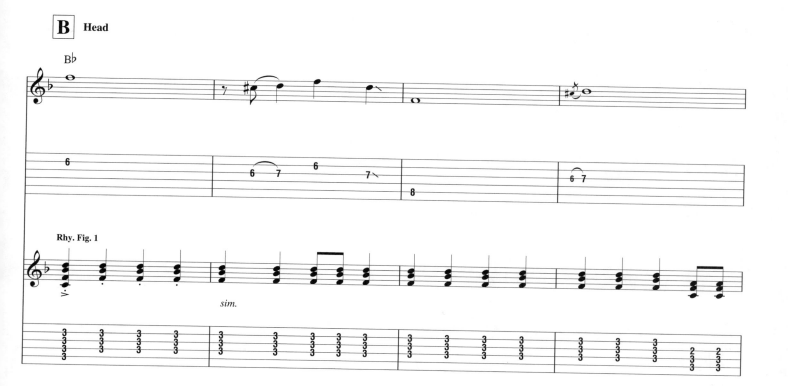

* T(6) = Thumb on 6th string.

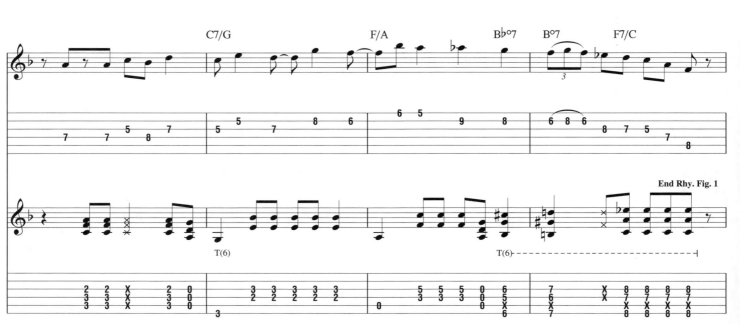

* Played behind the beat.

sim.

let ring -

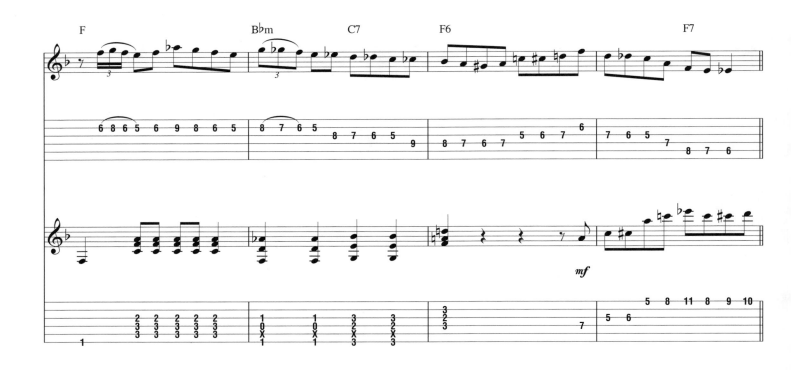

C **Guitar Solo**

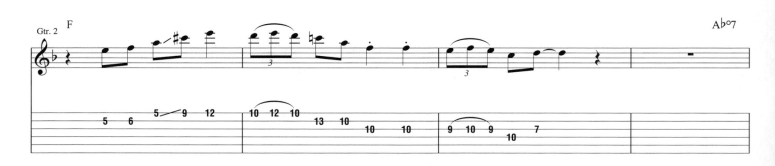

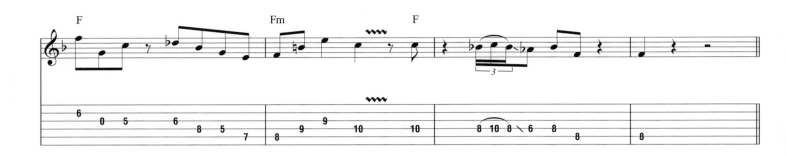

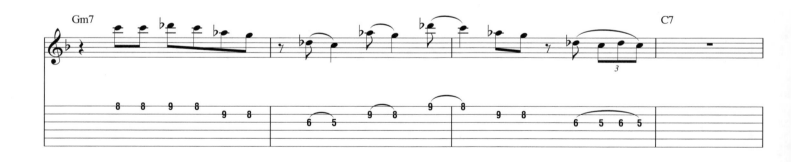

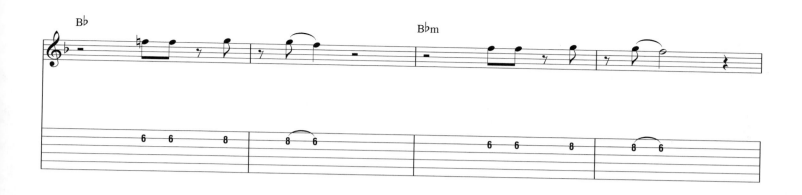

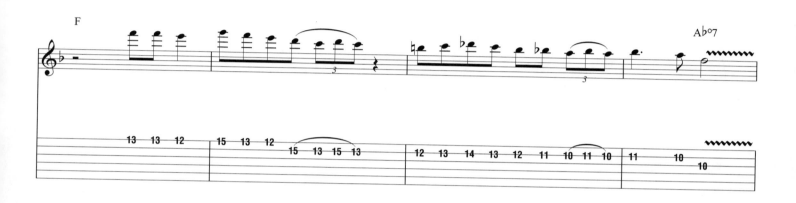

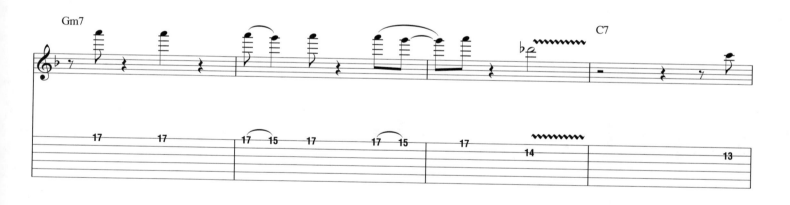

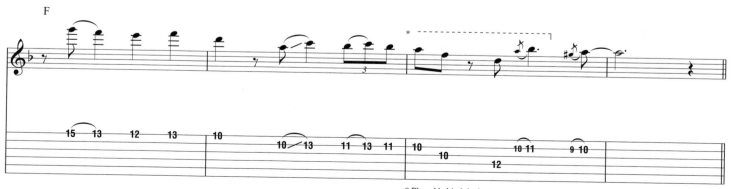

* Played behind the beat.

 **Violin Solo**

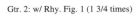

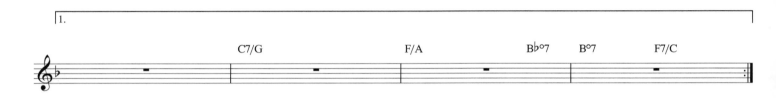

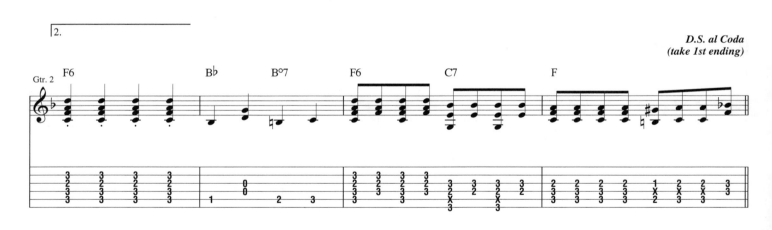

Coda

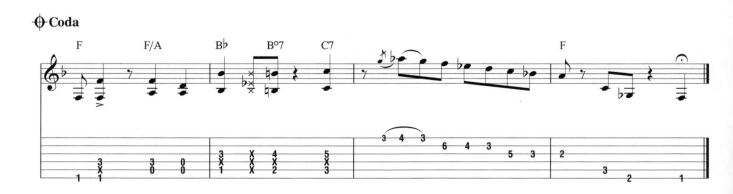

from *Jazz Masters 38*

Mélodie au Crépuscule

By Django Reinhardt

* Chord symbols reflect overall harmony.

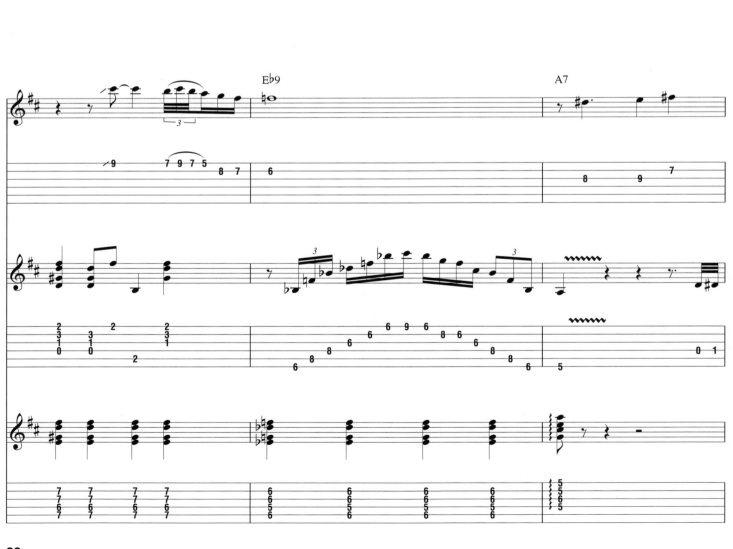

* T(5&6) = Thumb on 5th & 6th strings.

** T(6) = Thumb on 6th string.

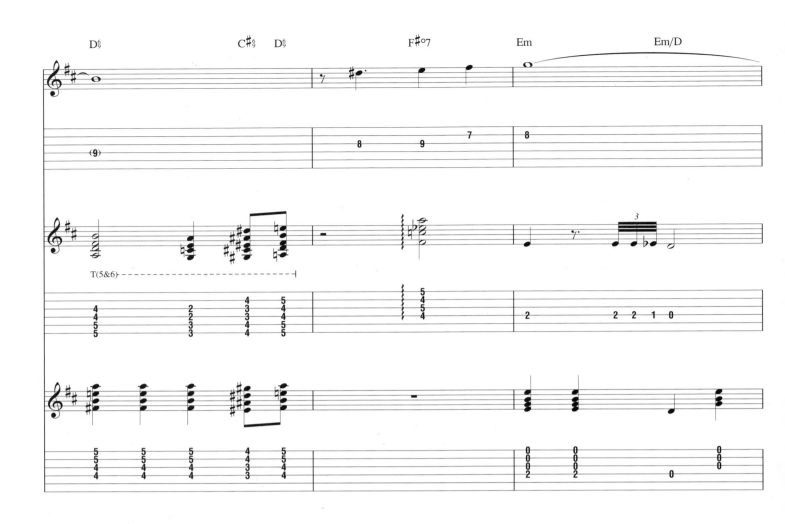

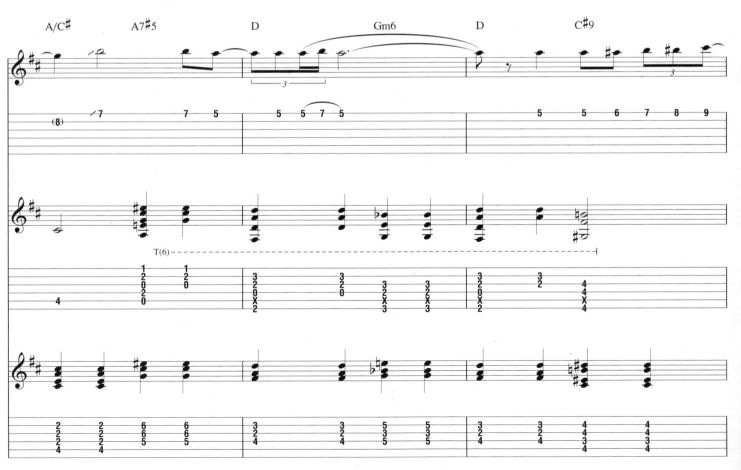

* Played behind the beat.

Guitar Solo
Gtr. 1 tacet

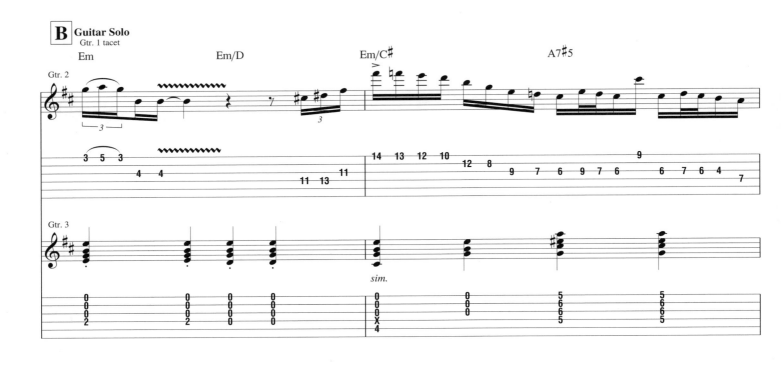

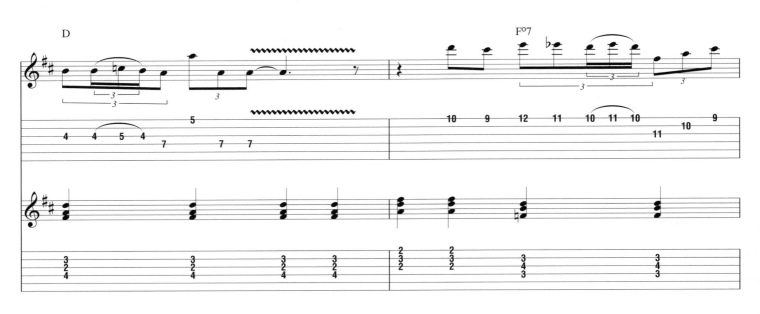

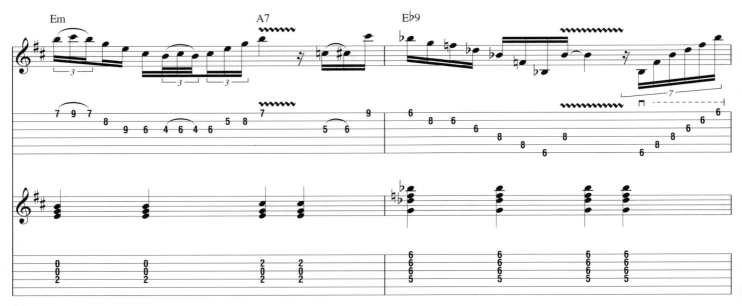

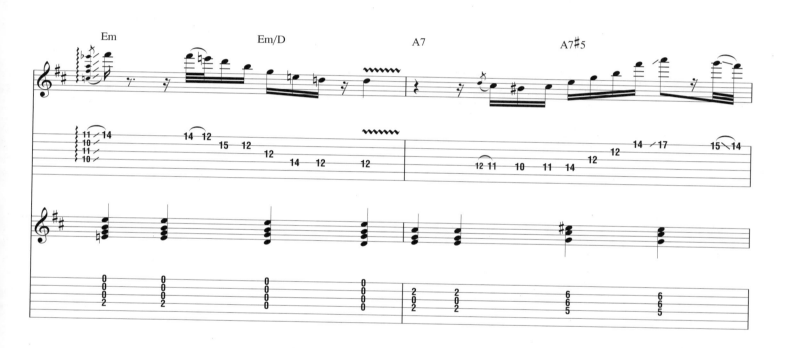

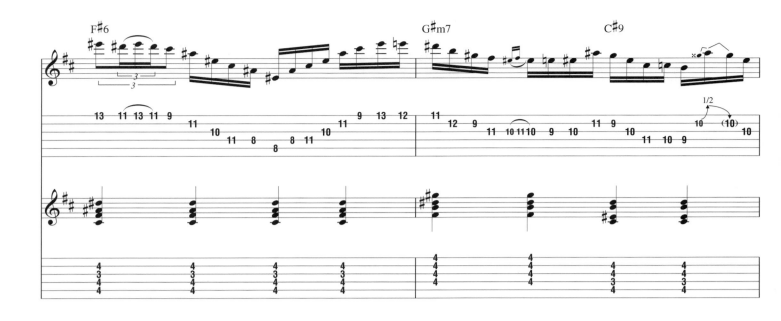

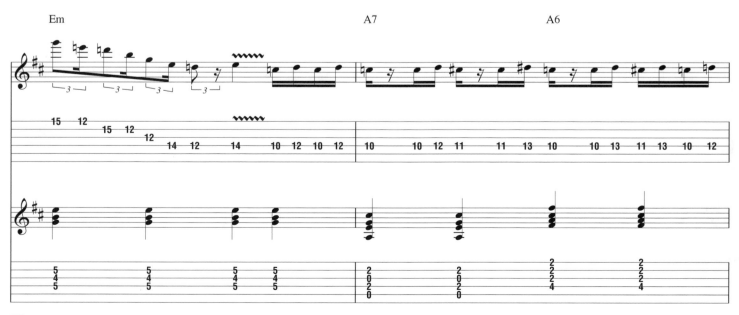

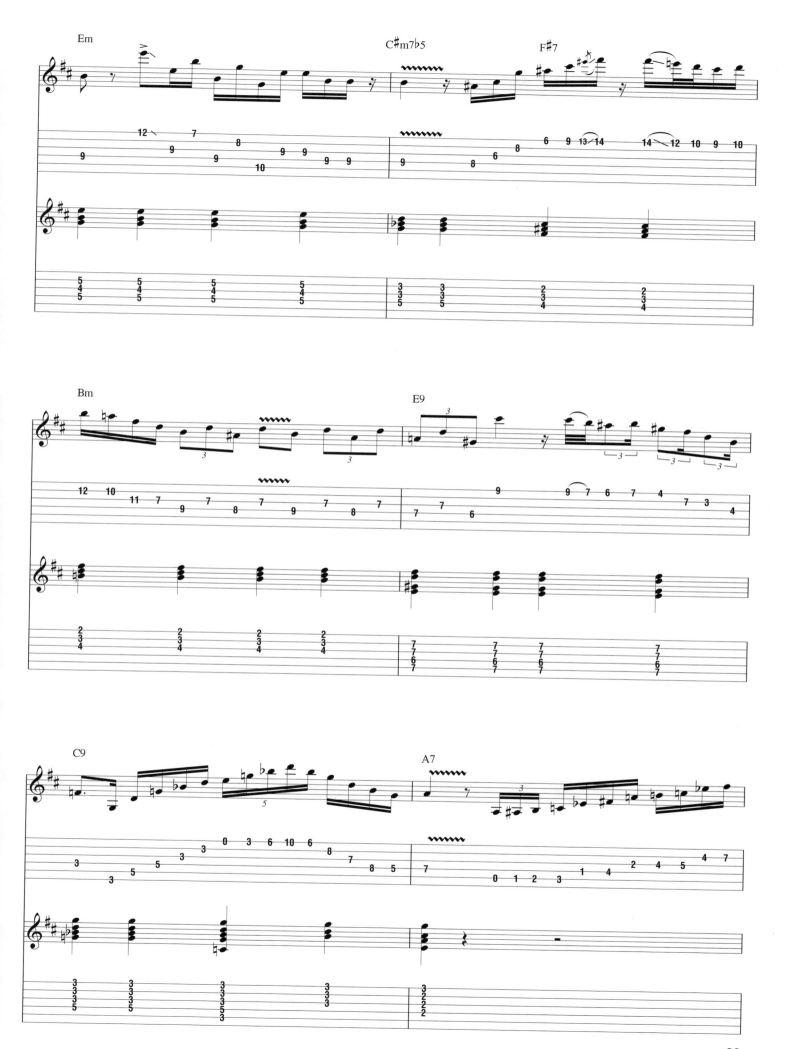

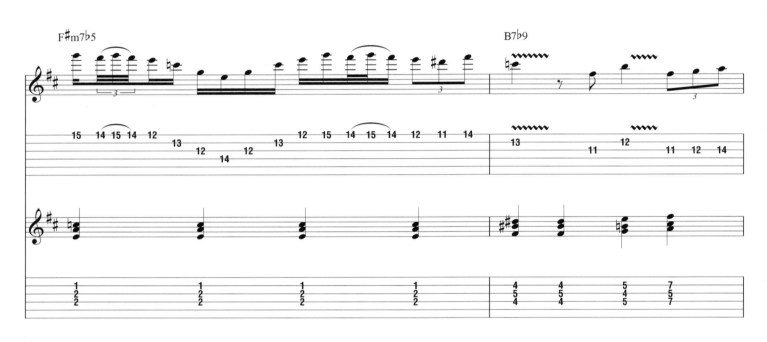

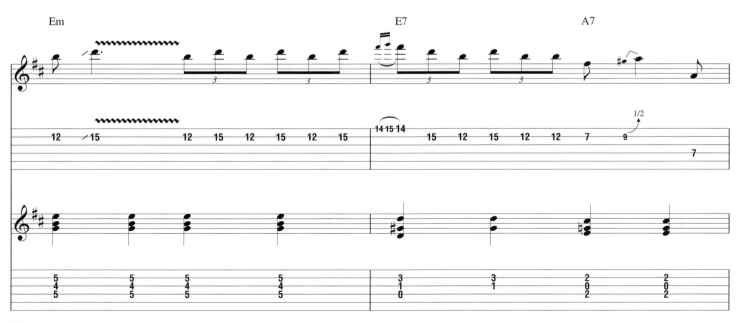

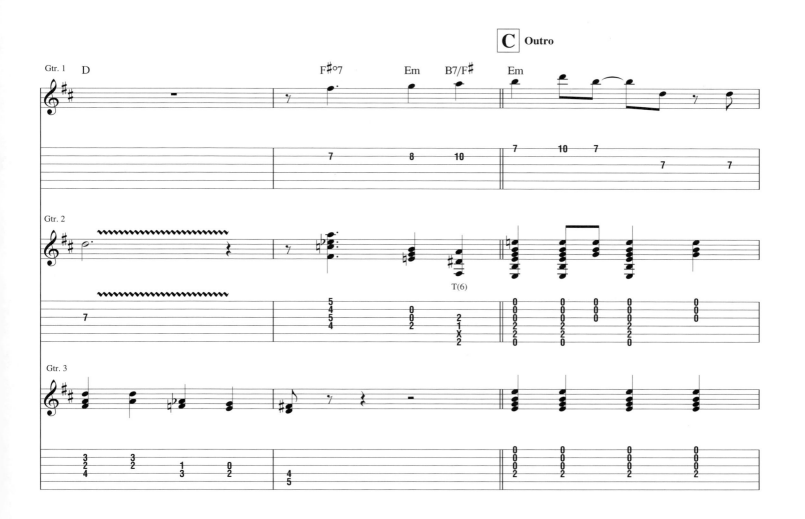

from *Djangology*
Minor Swing
By Django Reinhardt and Stephane Grappelli

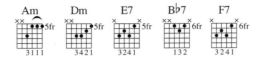

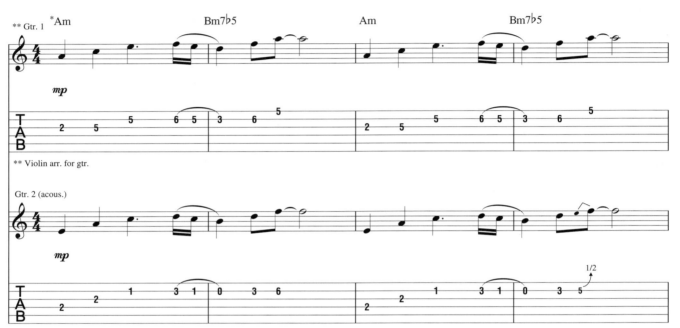

* Chord symbols reflect overall harmony.

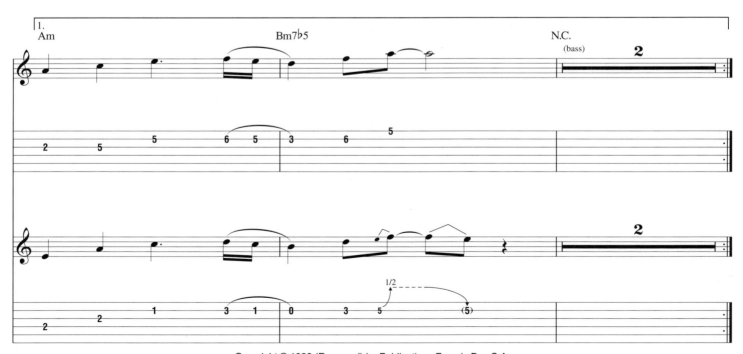

B Head

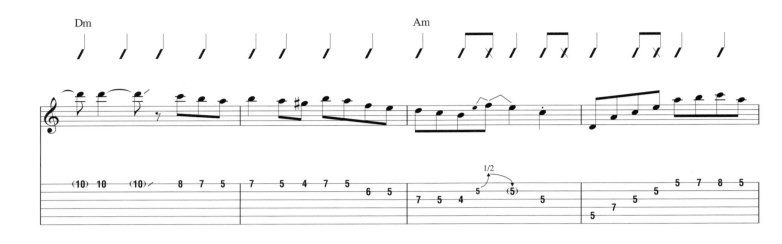

C **Guitar Solo**

Gtr. 3: w/ Rhy. Fig. 1 (3 times)

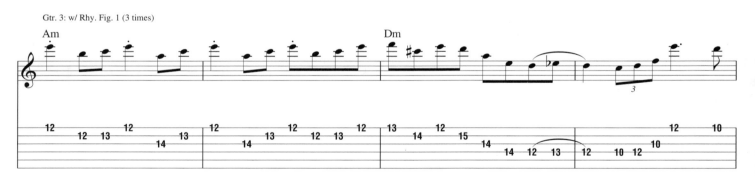

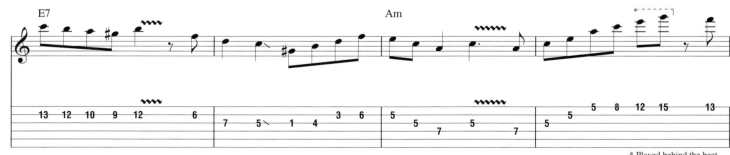

* Played behind the beat.

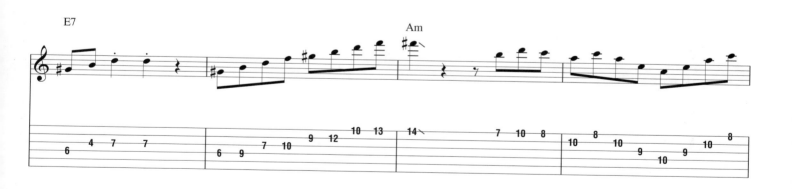
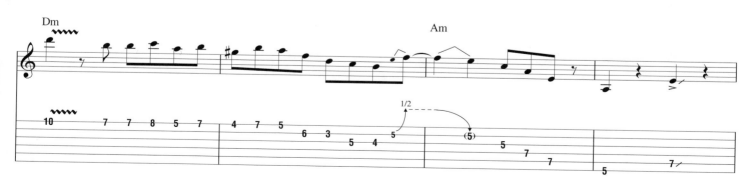

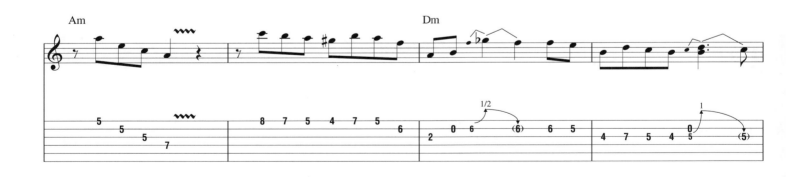

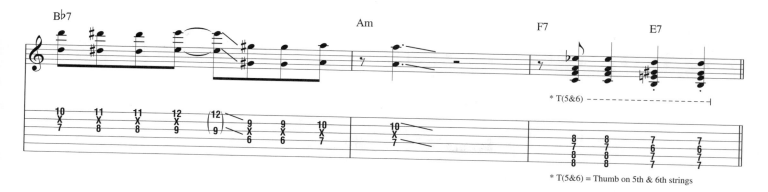

* T(5&6) = Thumb on 5th & 6th strings

D Violin Solo

Gtr. 3: w/ Rhy. Fig. 1 (4 times)

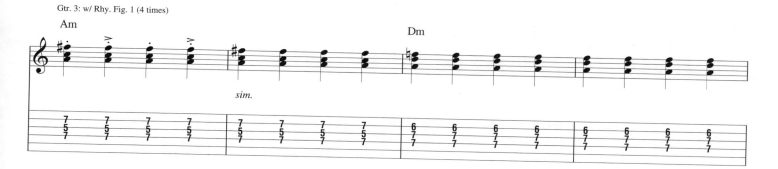

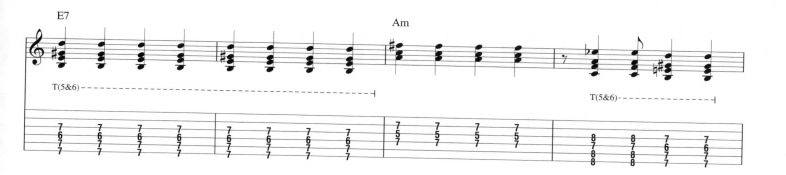

**T(6)=Thumb on 6th string.

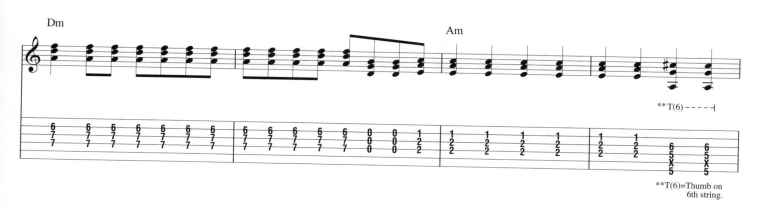

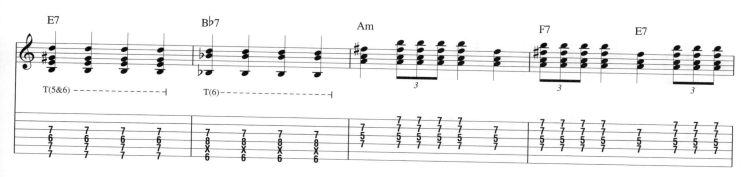

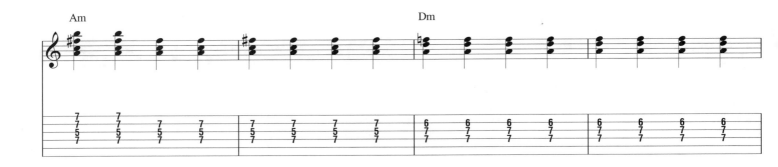
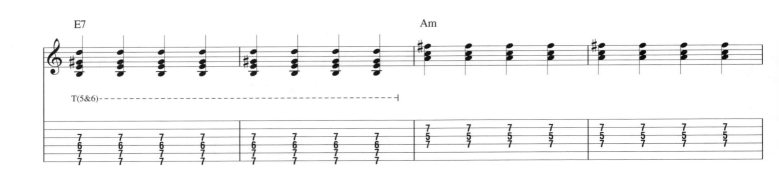
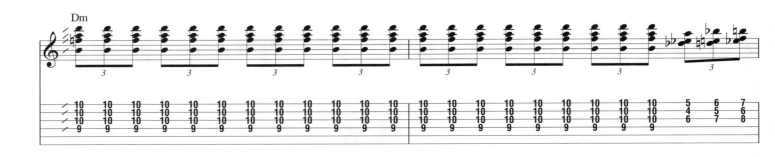
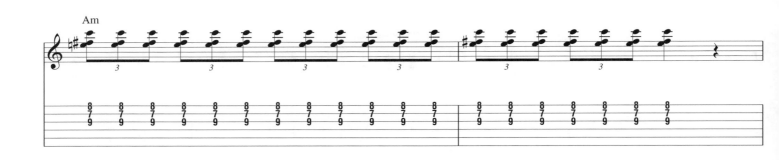
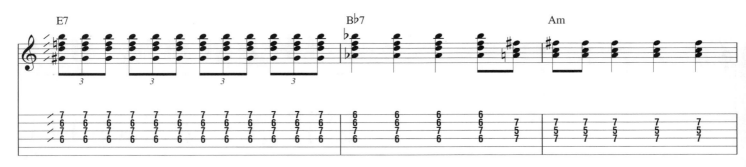

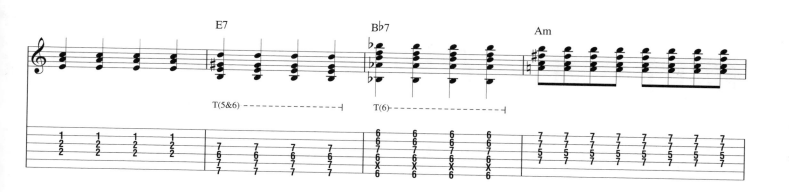

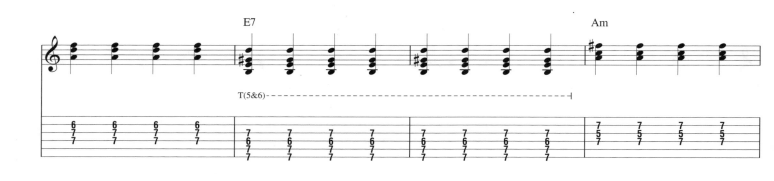
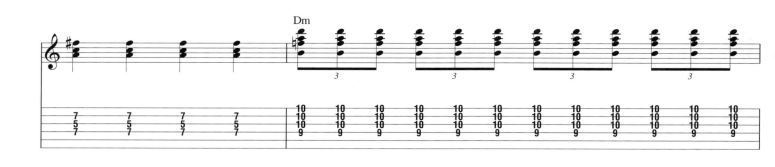
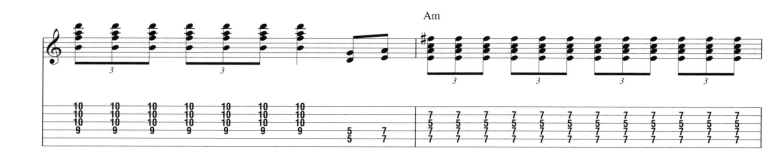
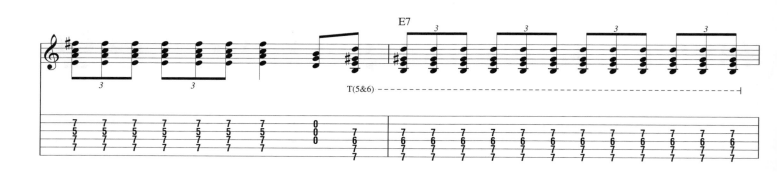
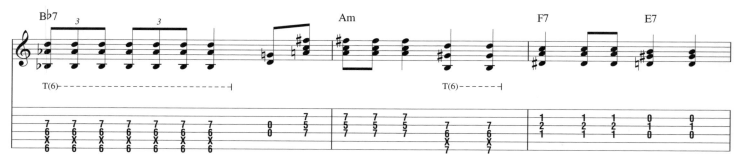

from *The Best of Django Reinhardt*

My Serenade

By Django Reinhardt

 Intro

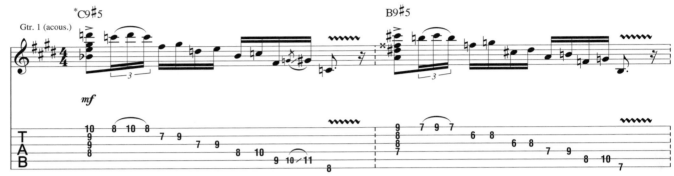

* Chord symbols reflect overall harmony.

 Head

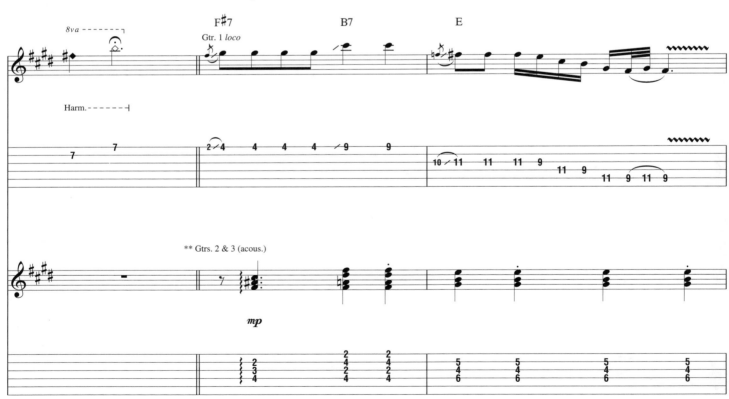

** Composite arrangement.

*T(6) = Thumb on 6th string.

Rhy. Fig. 1

103

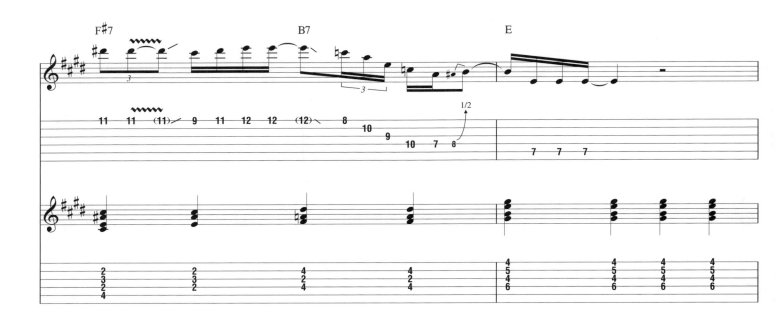

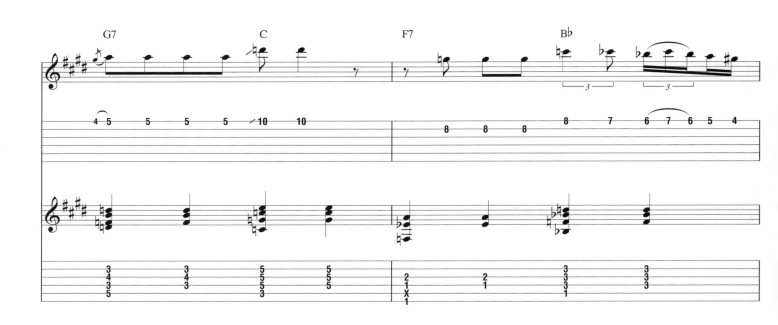

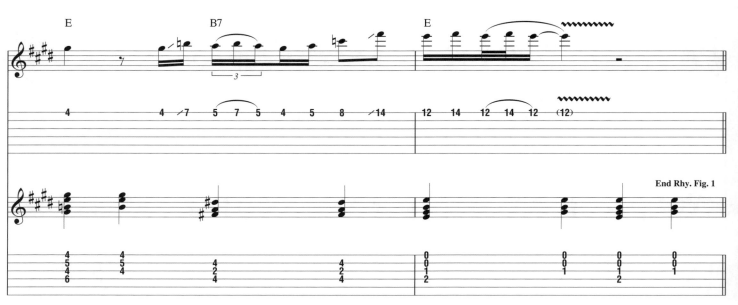

End Rhy. Fig. 1

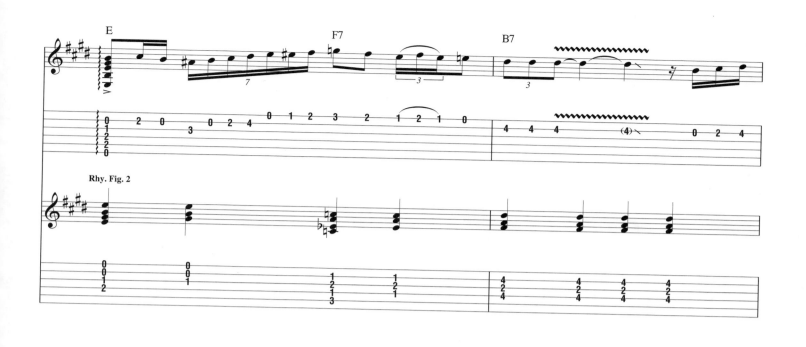

Rhy. Fig. 2

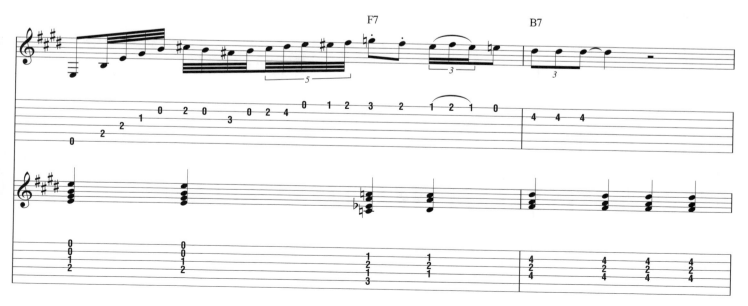

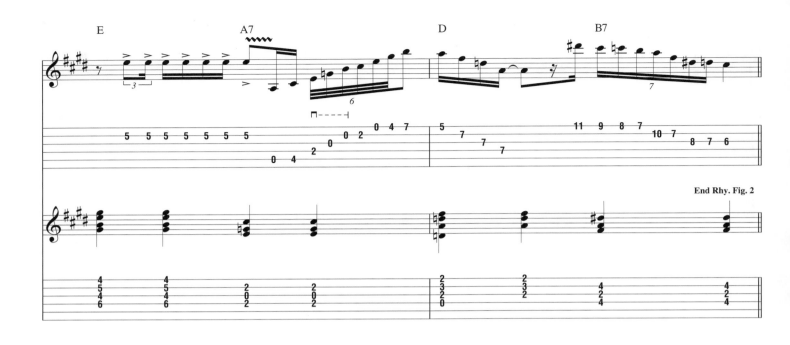

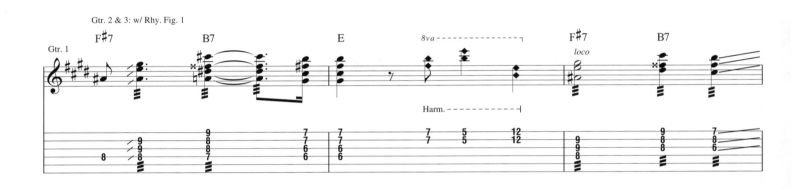

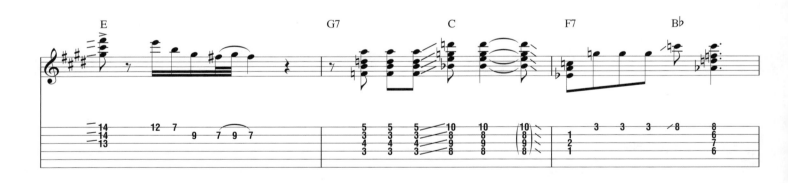

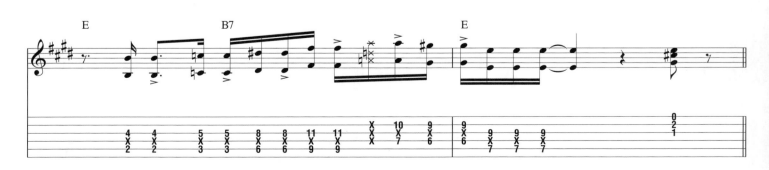

106

Violin Solo

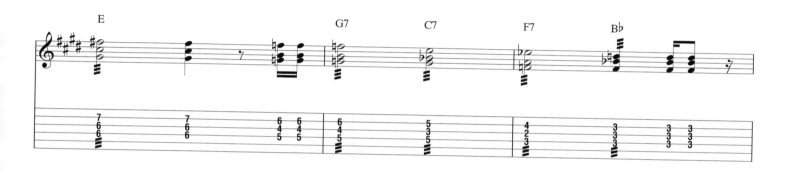

* T(4&5) = Thumb on 4th & 5th strings.

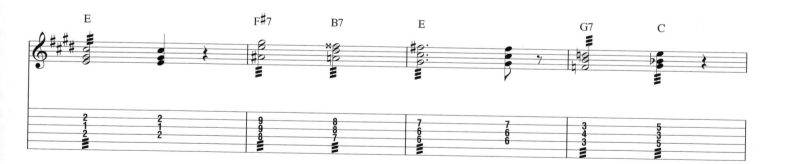

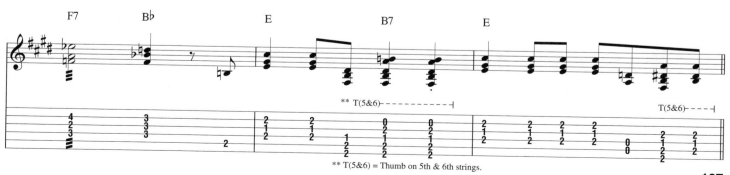

** T(5&6) = Thumb on 5th & 6th strings.

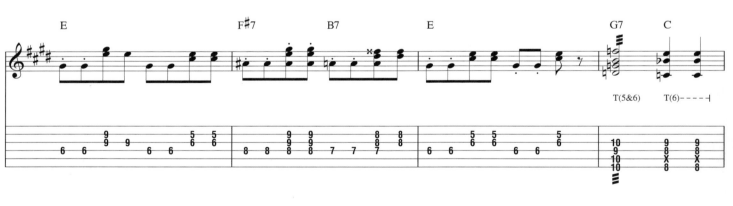

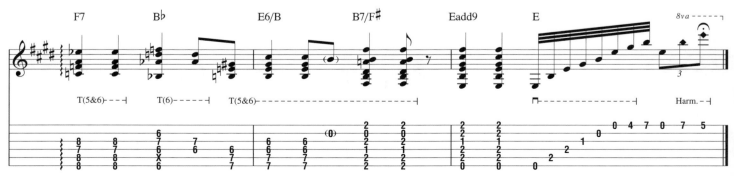

from *Djangology*

Nuages

By Django Reinhardt and Jacques Larue

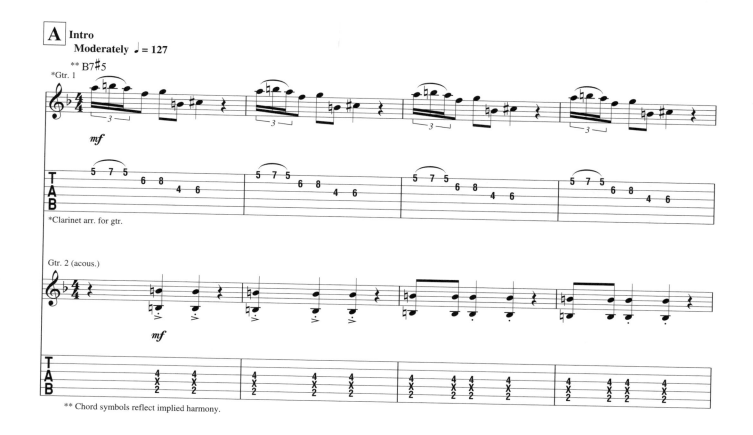

*Clarinet arr. for gtr.

** Chord symbols reflect implied harmony.

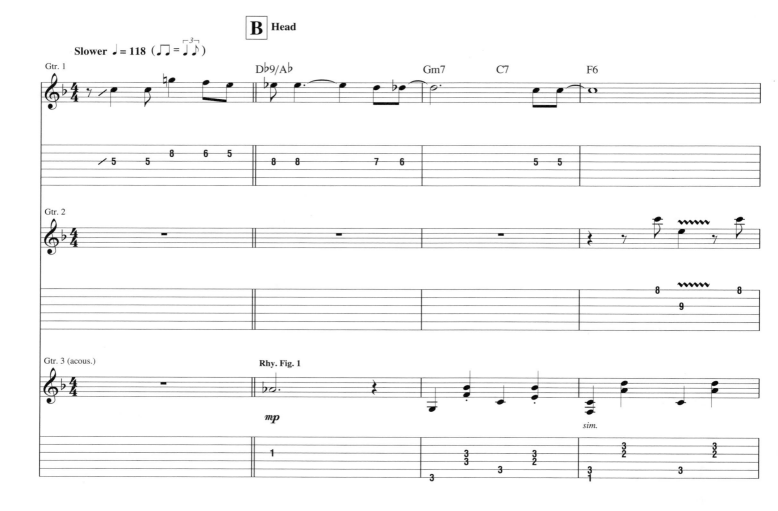

*T(6) = Thumb on 6th string.

End Rhy. Fig. 2

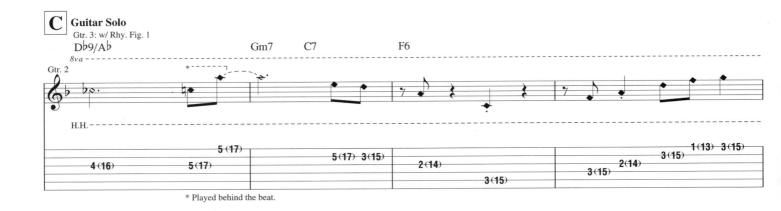

* Played behind the beat.

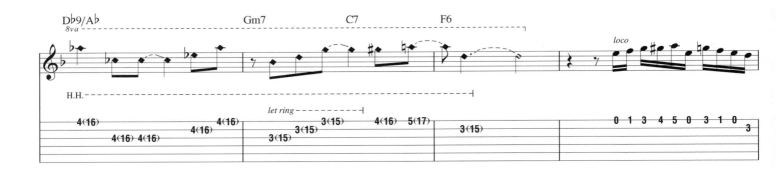

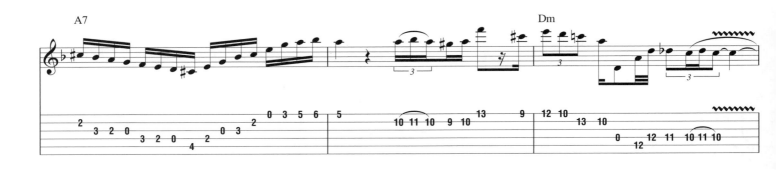

**Played as even eighth notes.

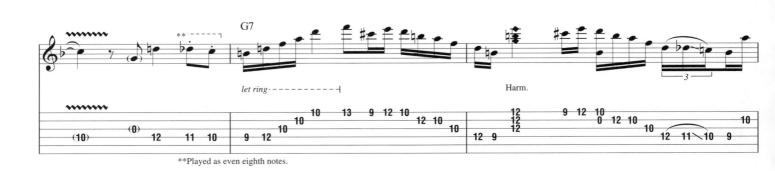

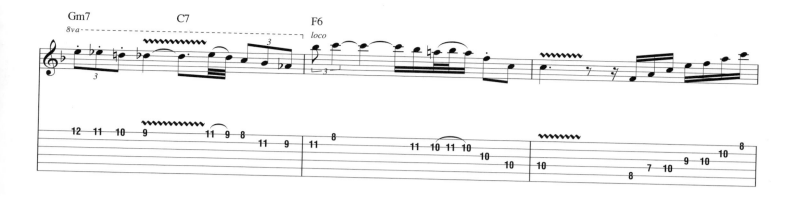

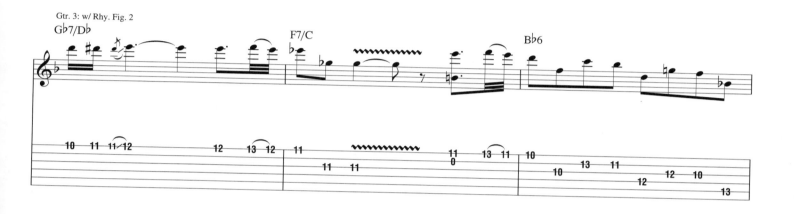

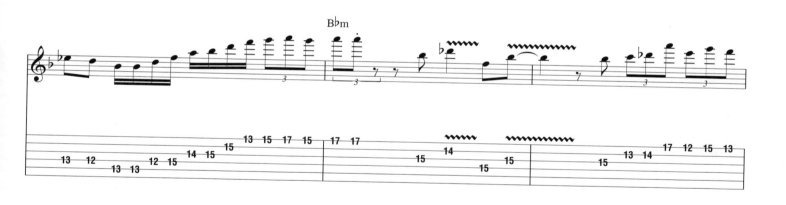

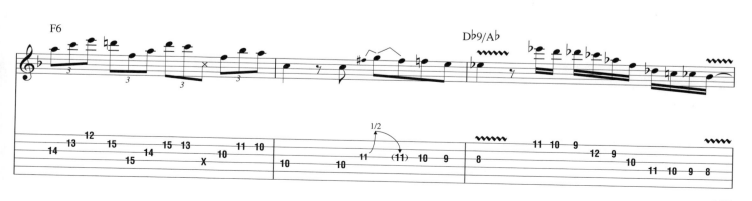

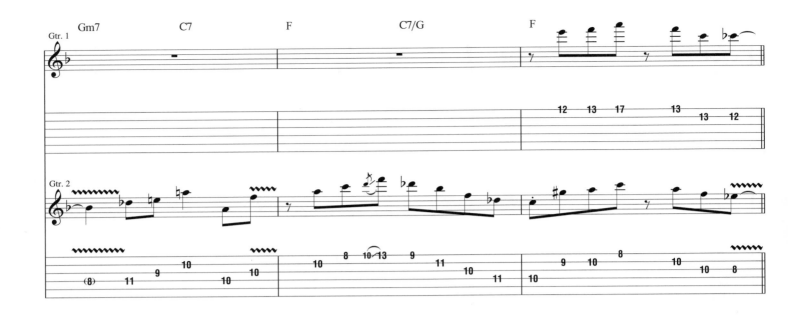

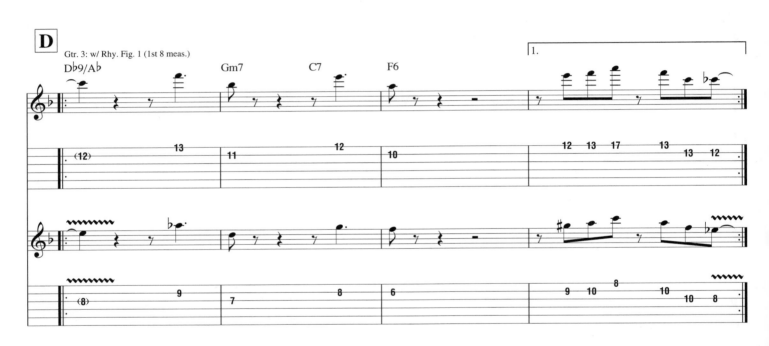

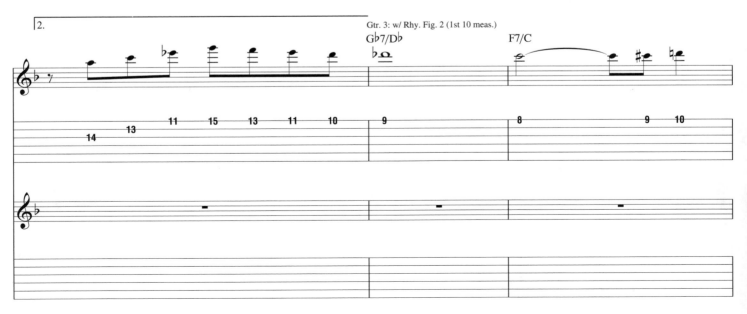

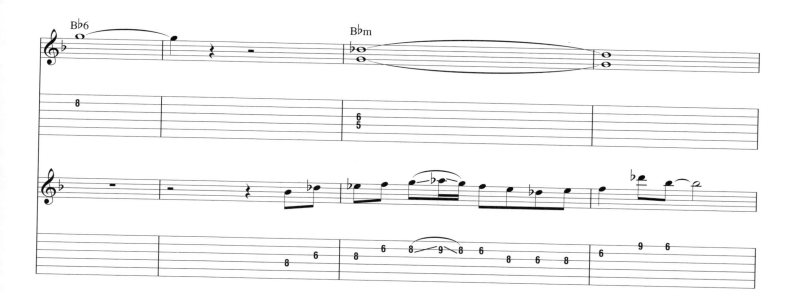

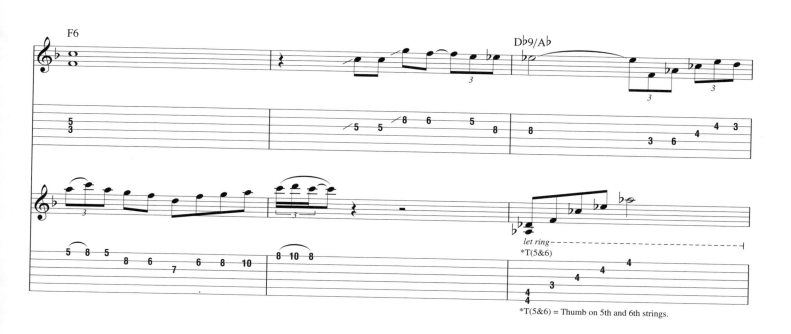

*T(5&6) = Thumb on 5th and 6th strings.

Old Folks at Home
(Swanee River)

Words and Music by Stephen C. Foster

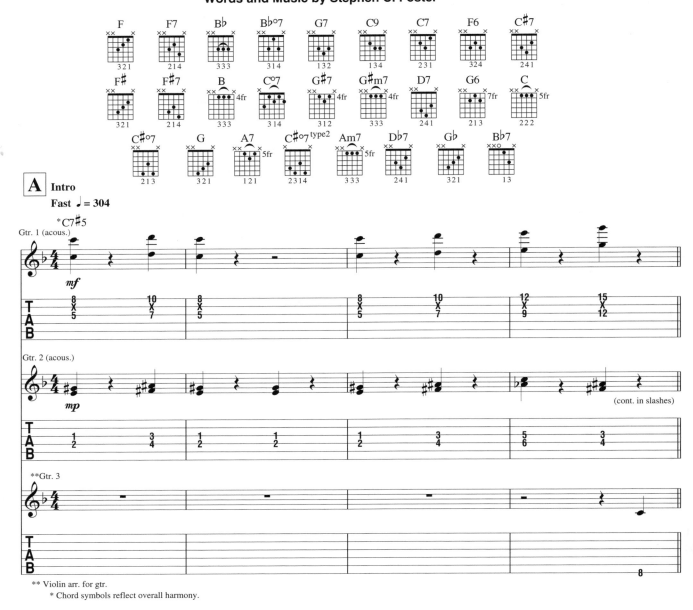

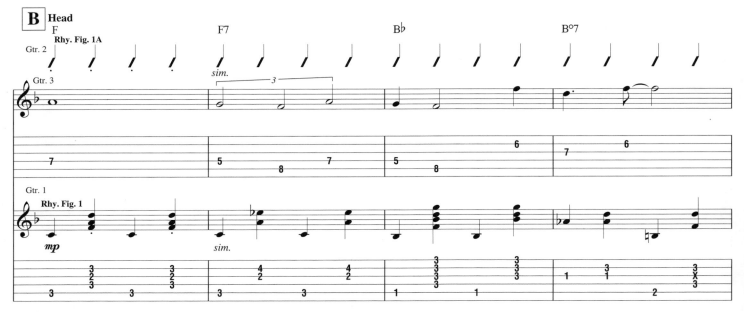

* T(5&6) = Thumb on 5th & 6th strings.

**T(6) = Thumb on 6th string.

F Guitar Solo

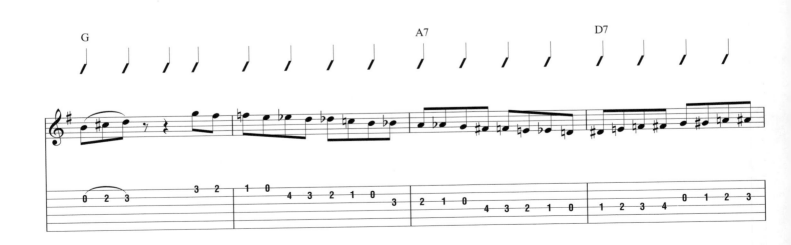

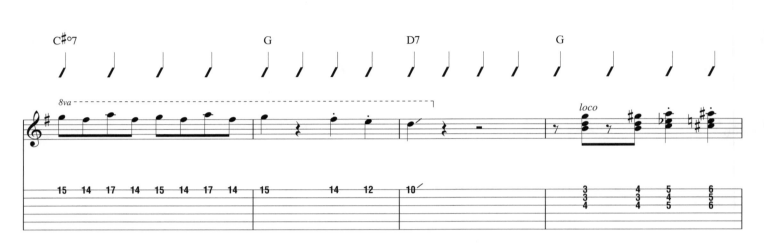

D.S. al Coda
(take repeats)

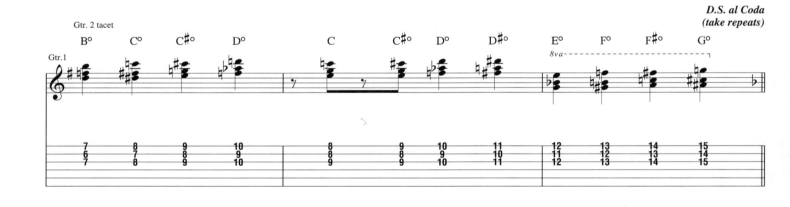

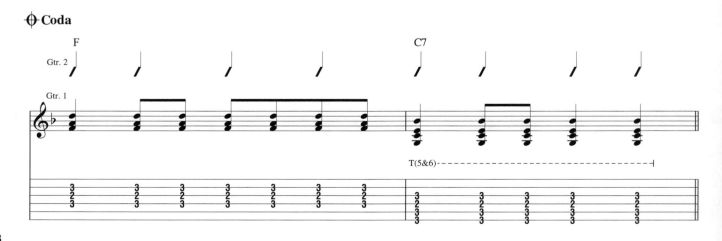

from *Djangology*

Rose Room

Words by Harry Williams
Music by Art Hickman

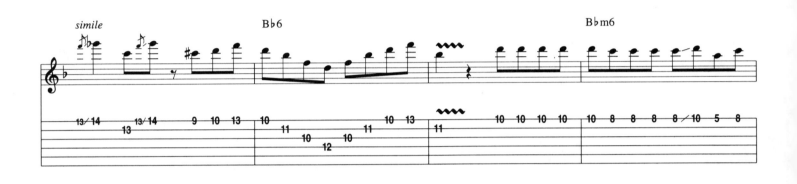

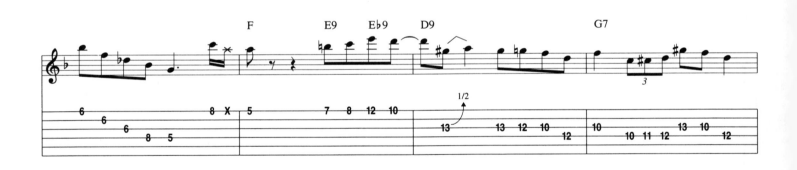

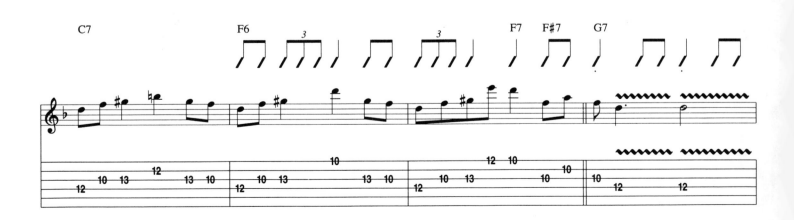

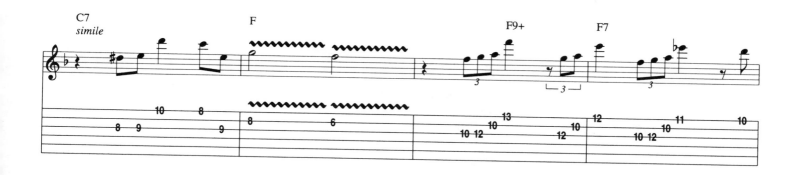

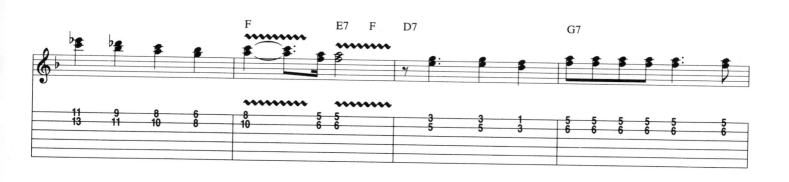

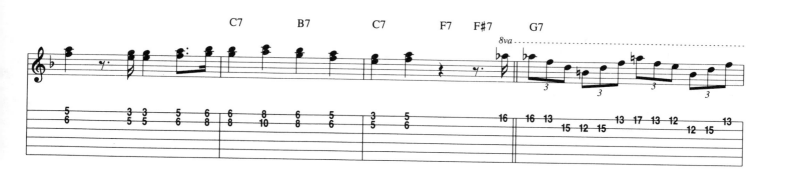

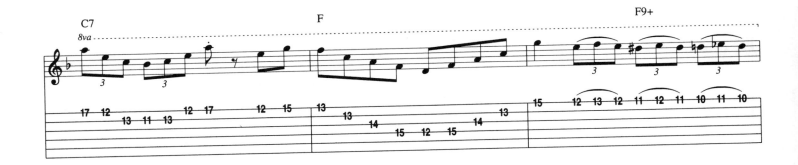

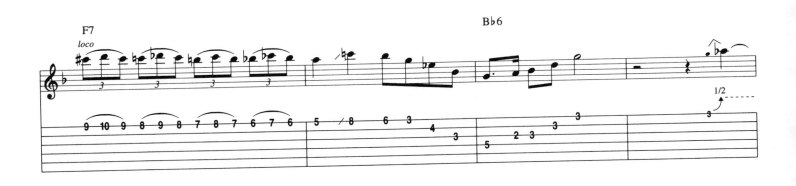

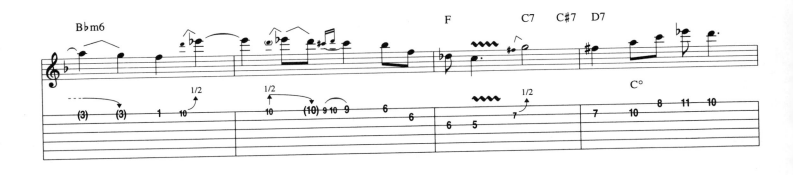

from *The Very Best of 1934-1939*

Stardust
Words by Mitchell Parish
Music by Hoagy Carmichael

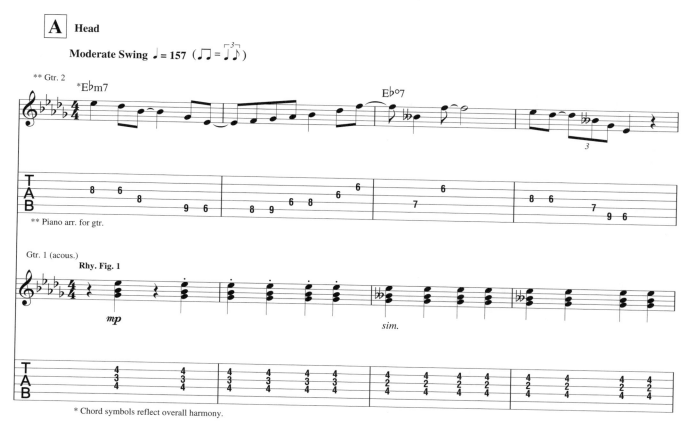

* Chord symbols reflect overall harmony.

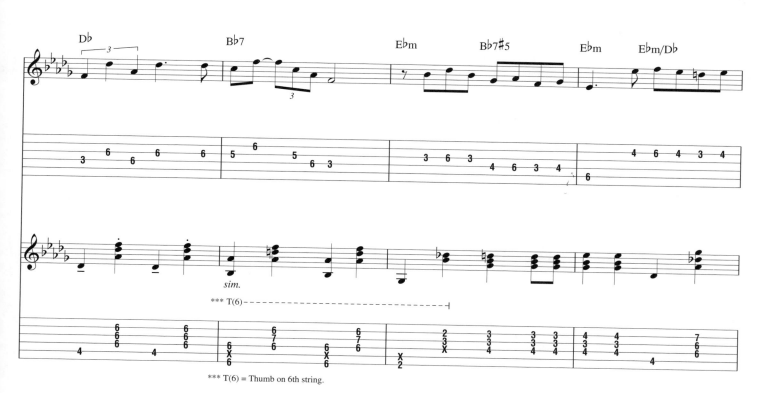

*** T(6) = Thumb on 6th string.

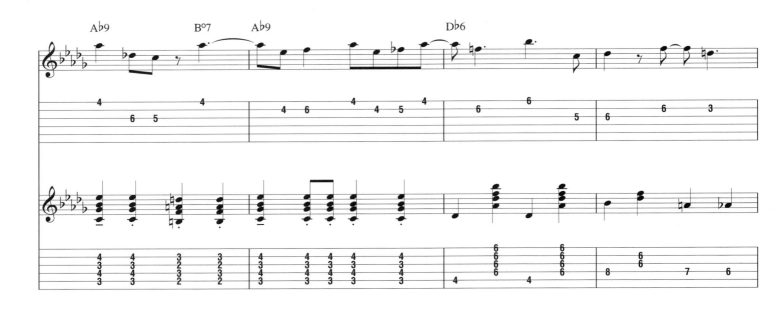

* T(5&6) = Thumb on
  5th & 6th strings.

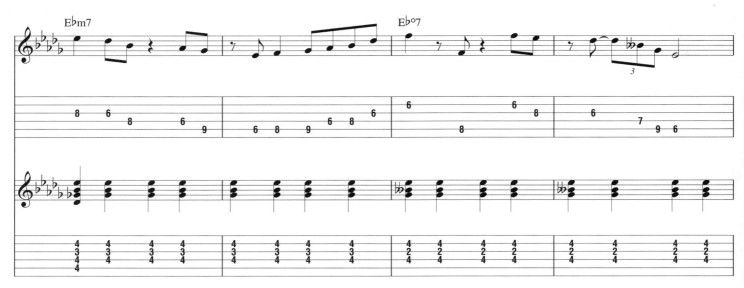

from *Djangology*

Swing 42

By Django Reinhardt

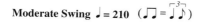

*Chord symbols reflect overall harmony.

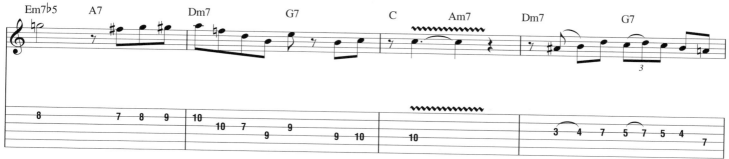

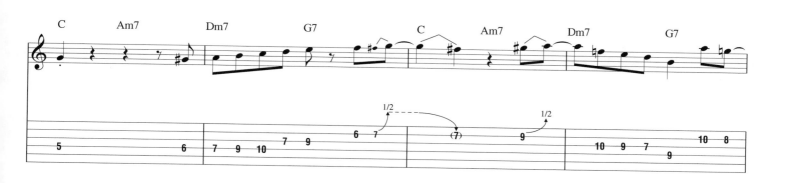

**T (6) = Thumb on
6th string.

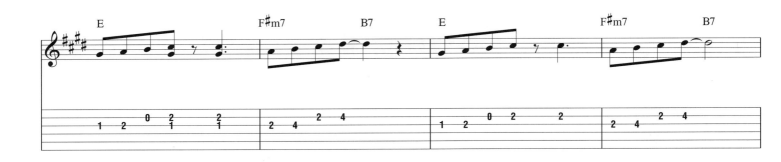

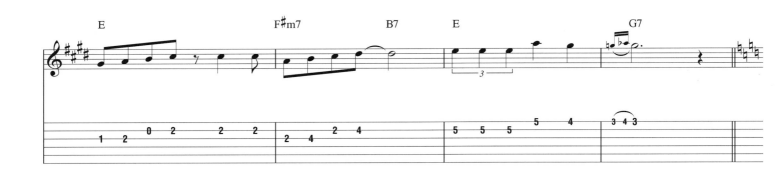

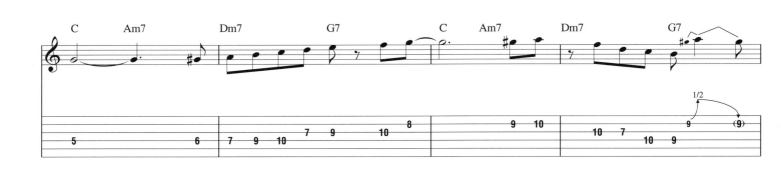

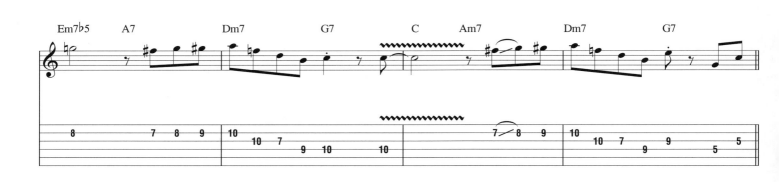

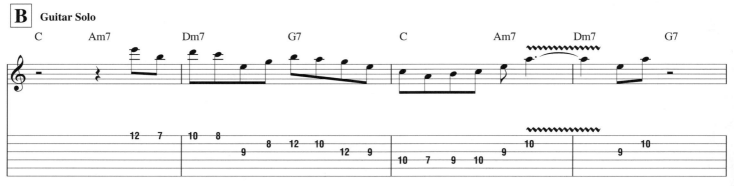

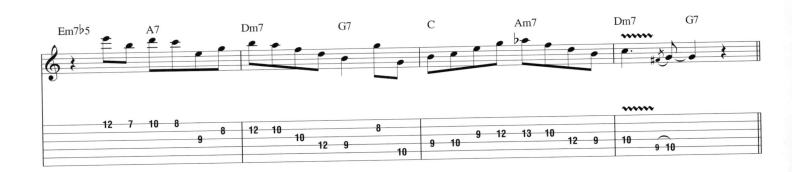

C **Clarinet Solo**

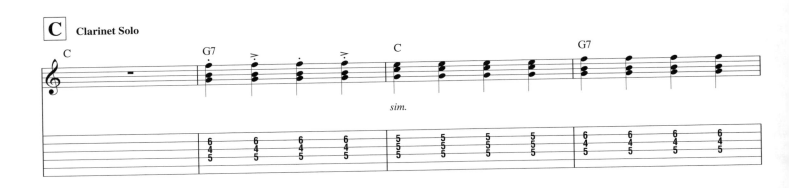

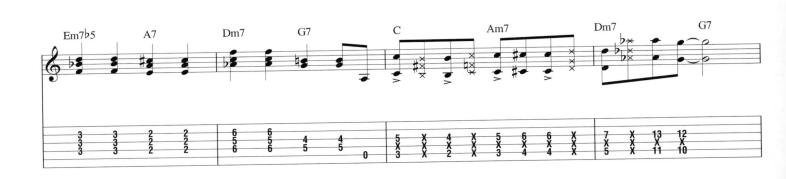

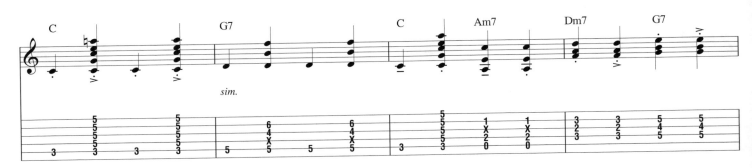

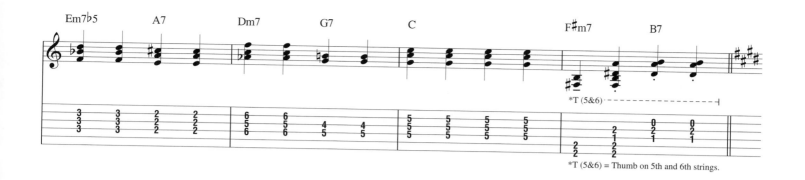

*T (5&6) = Thumb on 5th and 6th strings.

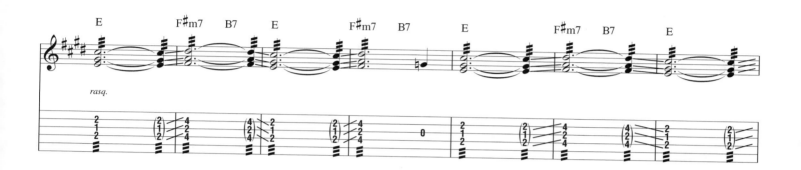

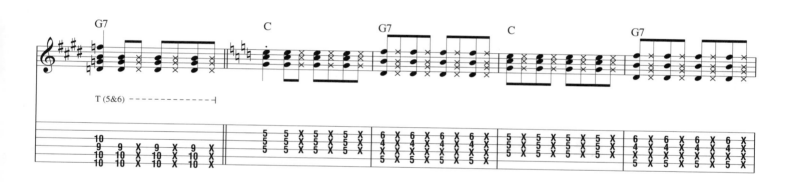

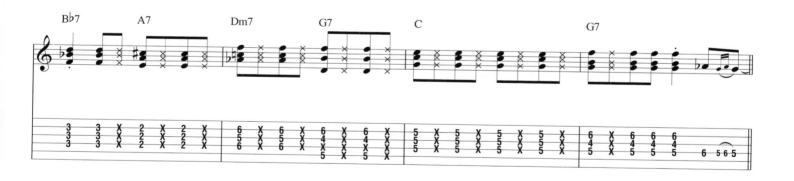

D Head

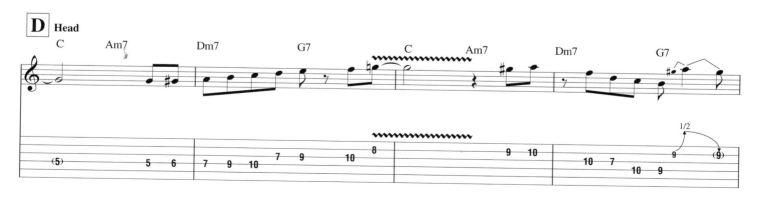

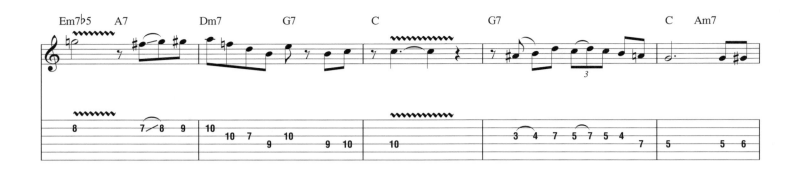
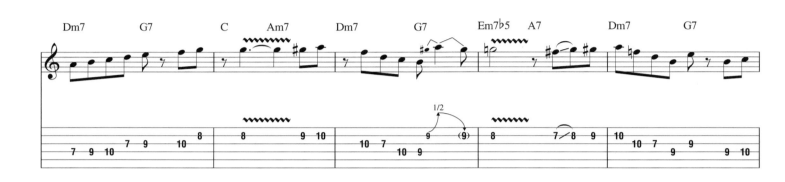
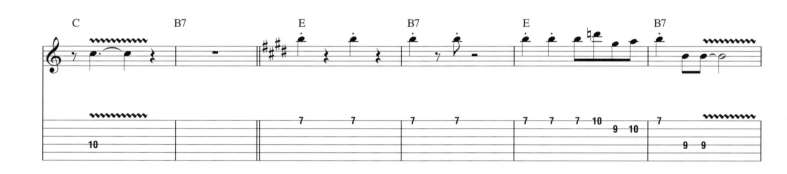
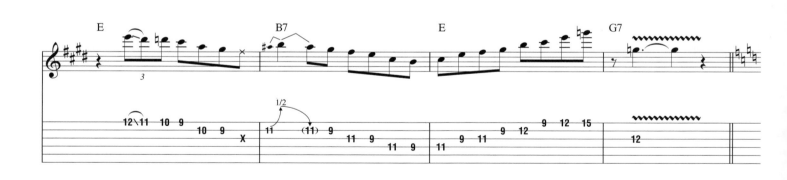
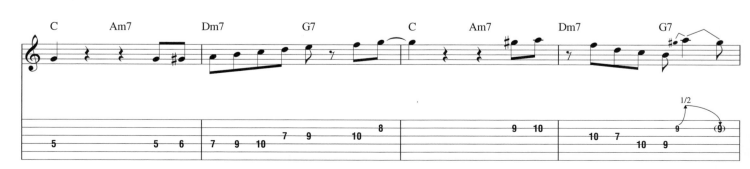

from *Djangology*

Swing Guitar

By Django Reinhardt and Stephane Grappelli

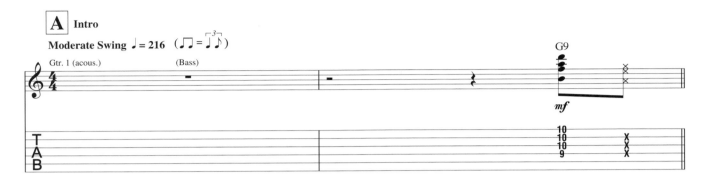

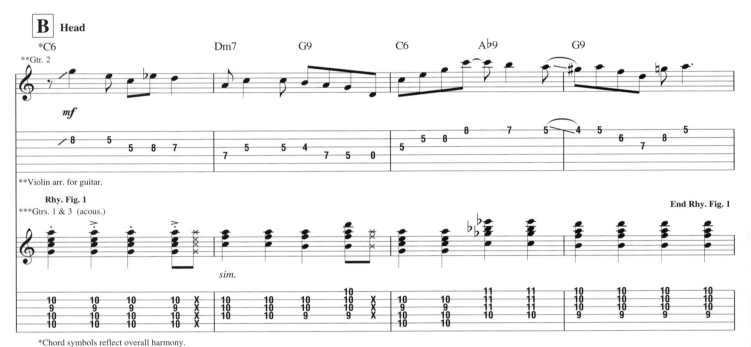

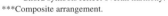

*Violin arr. for guitar.

*Chord symbols reflect overall harmony.
***Composite arrangement.

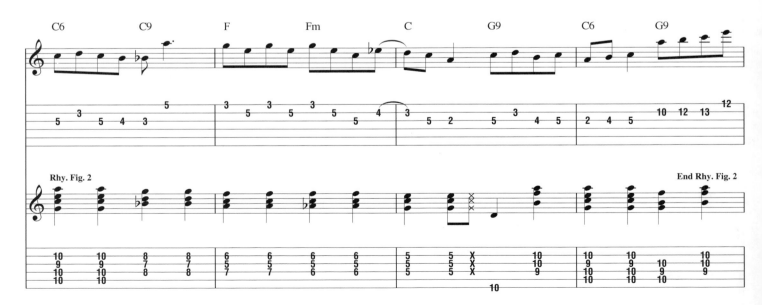

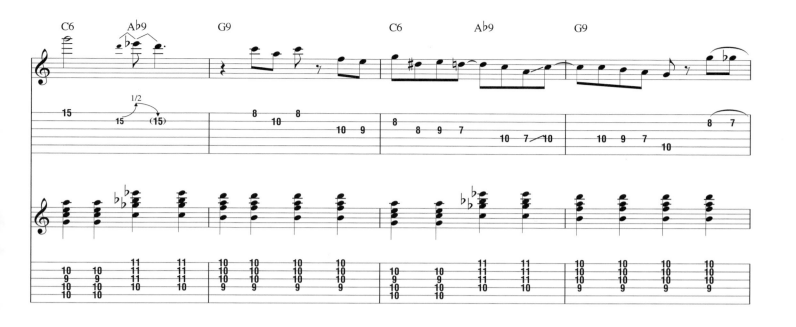

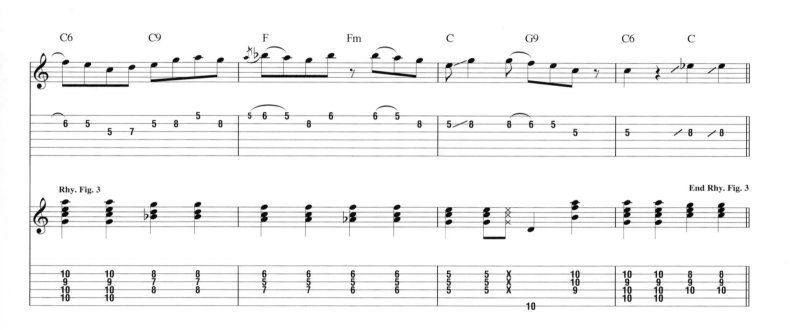

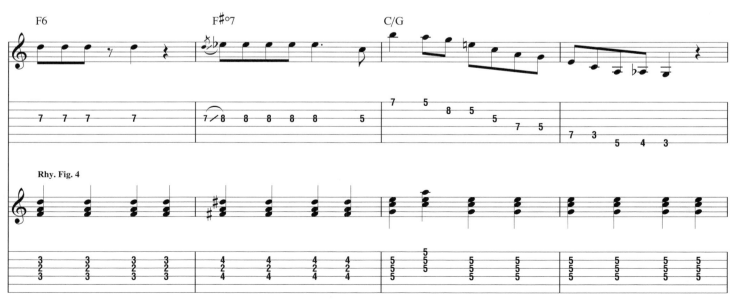

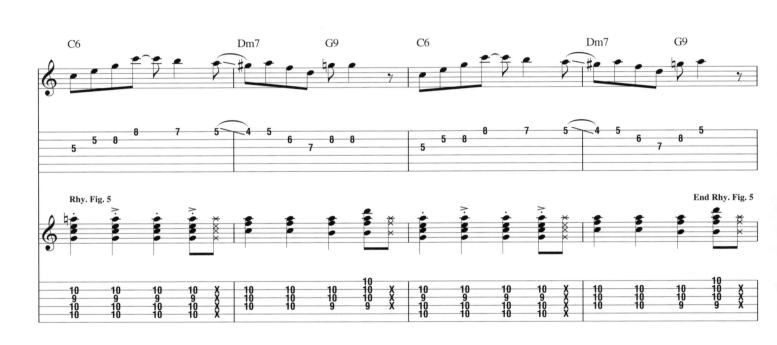

148

149

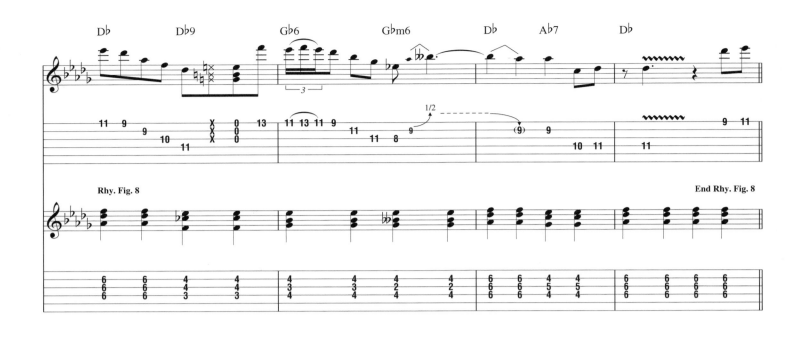

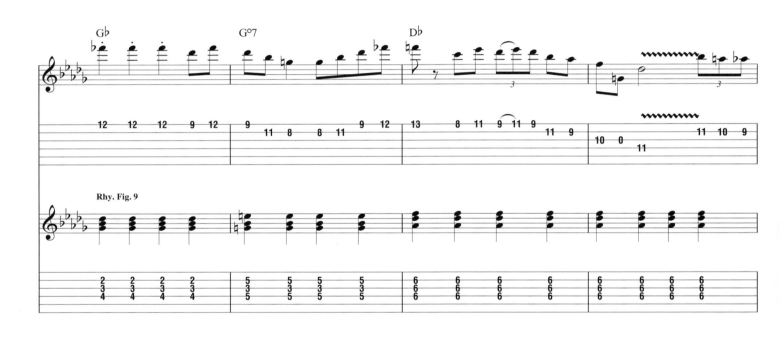

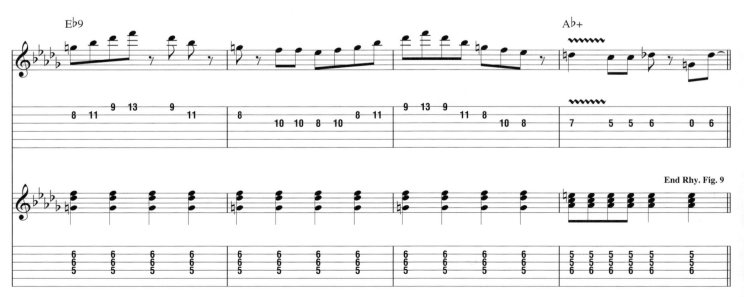

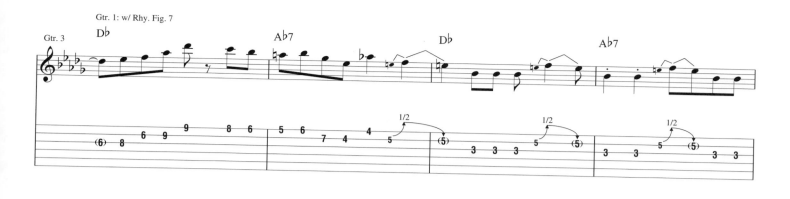

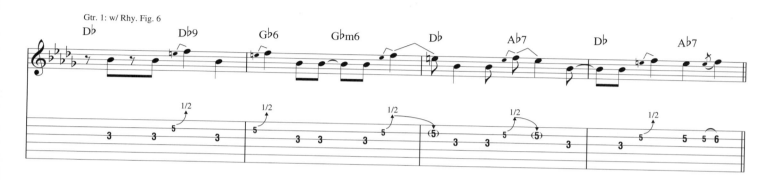

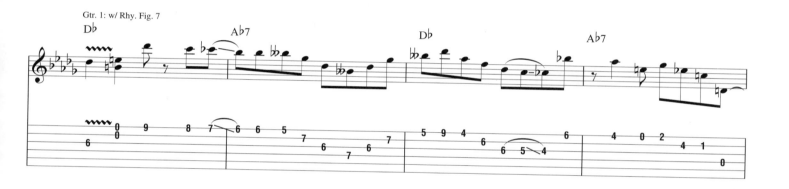

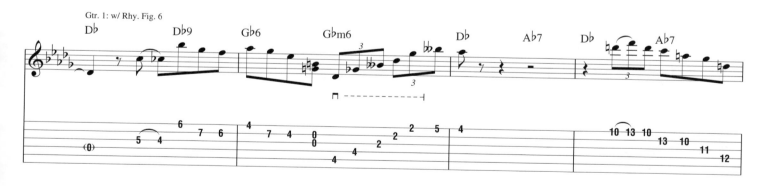

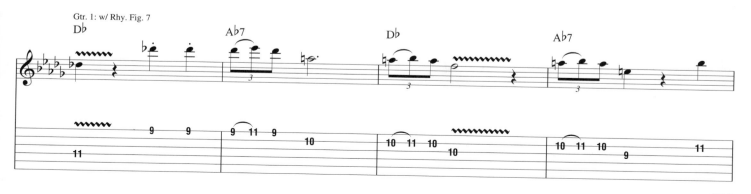

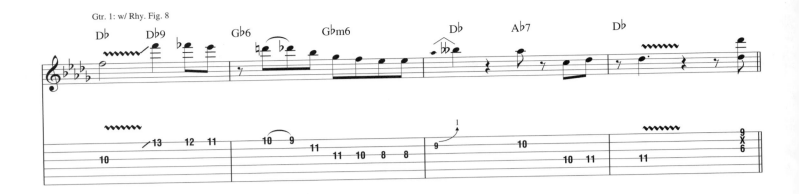

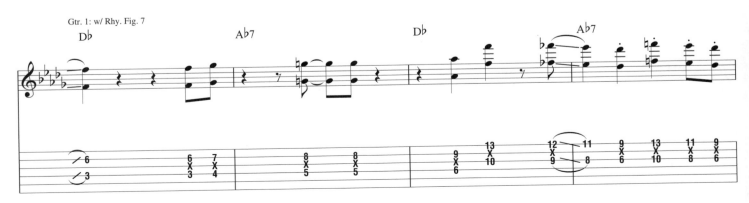

D Violin Solo

from *The Very Best of 1934-1939*

Tiger Rag
(Hold That Tiger)

Words by Harry DeCosta
Music by Original Dixieland Jazz Band

*Chord symbols reflect overall harmony.

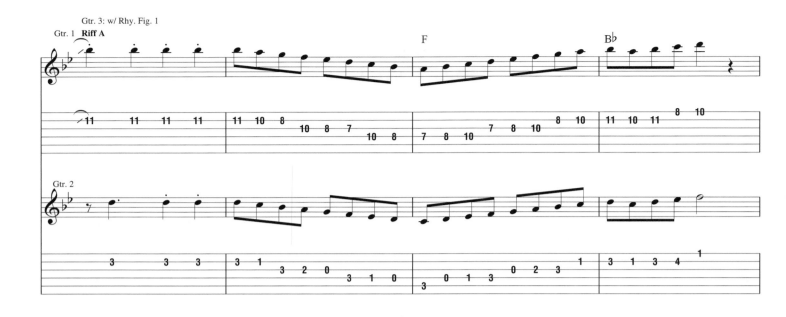

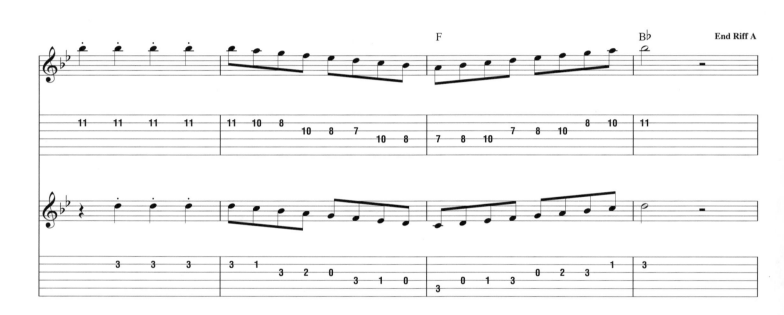

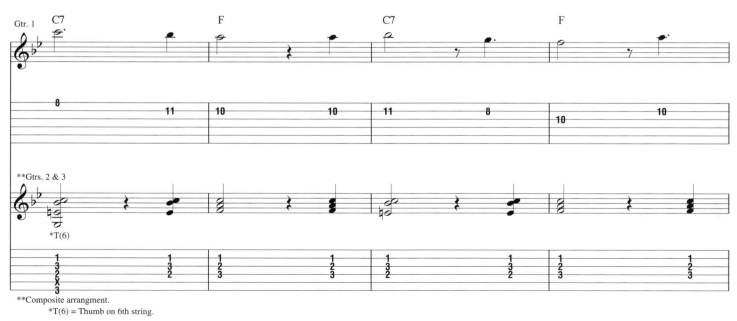

**Composite arrangment.
*T(6) = Thumb on 6th string.

Gtrs. 1 & 3: w/ Riff A & Rhy. Fig. 1

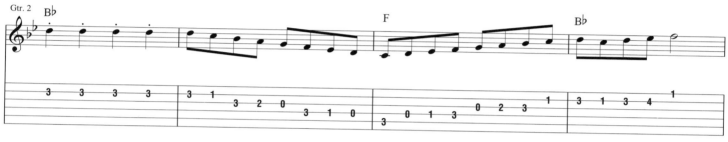

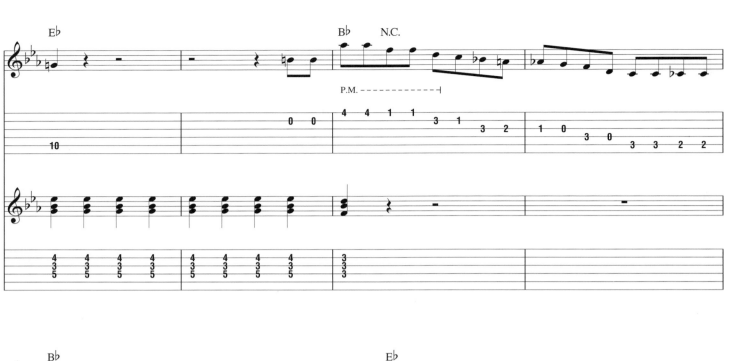

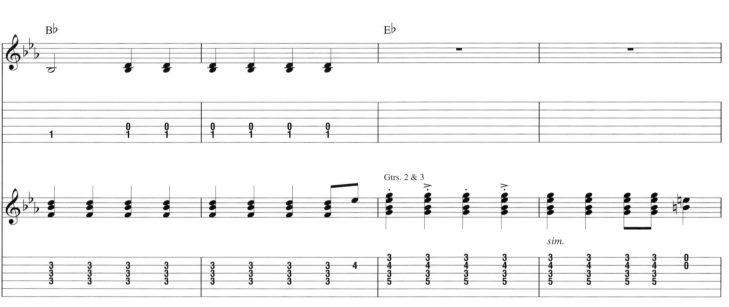

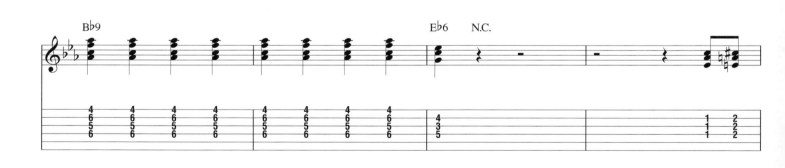

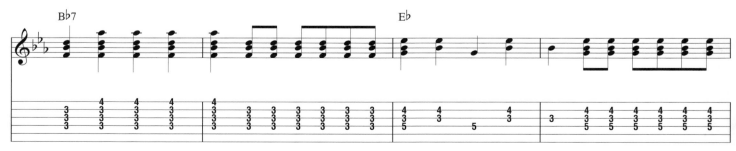

*T(5&6)=Thumb on 5th & 6th strings.

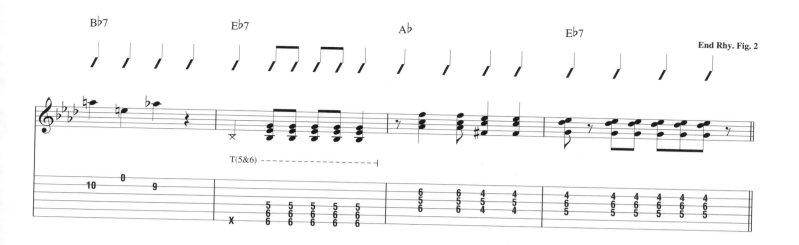

D Violin Solo

1st time, Gtr. 3: w/ Rhy. Fig. 2
2nd time, Gtr. 3: w/ Rhy Fig. 2 (1st 30 meas.)

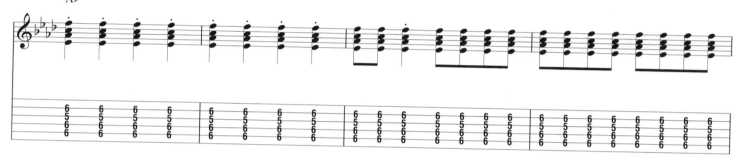

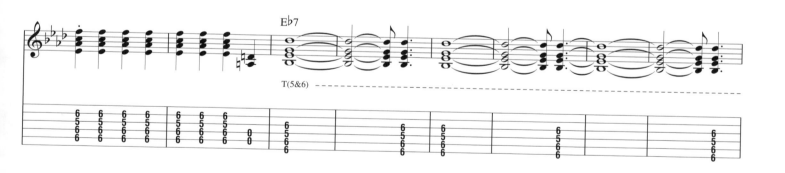

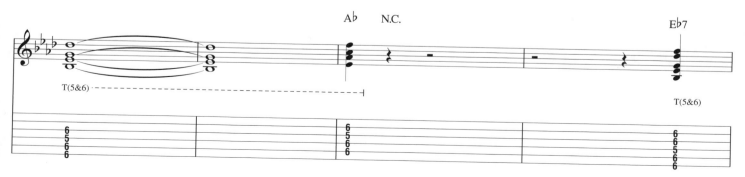

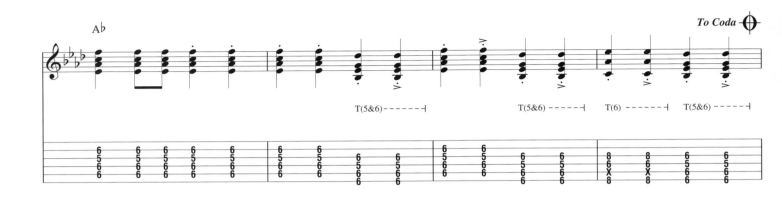

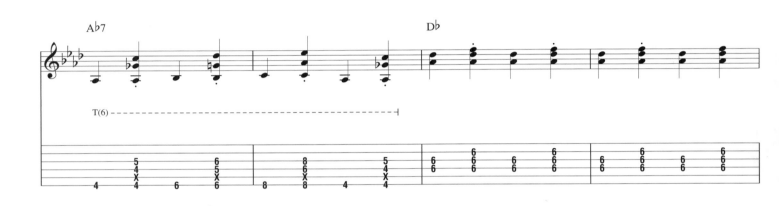

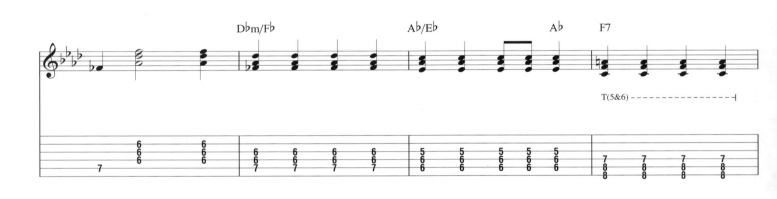

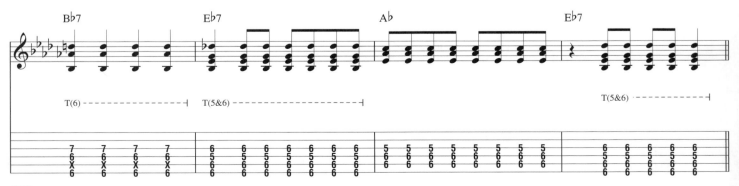

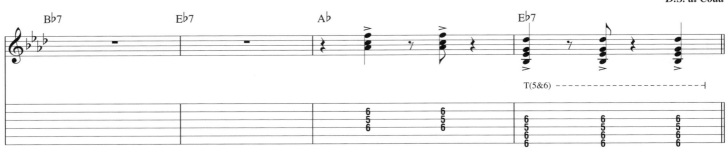

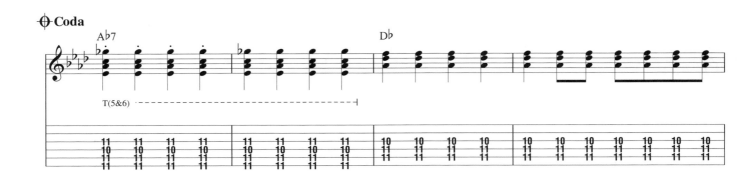

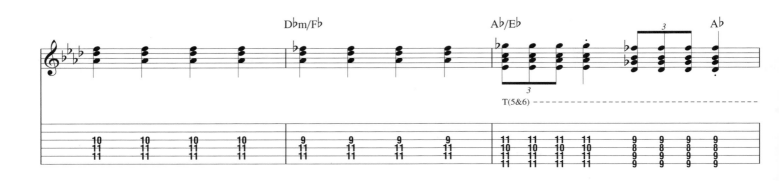

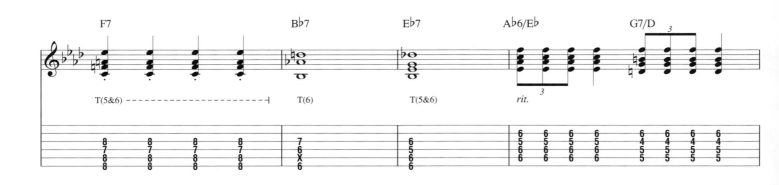

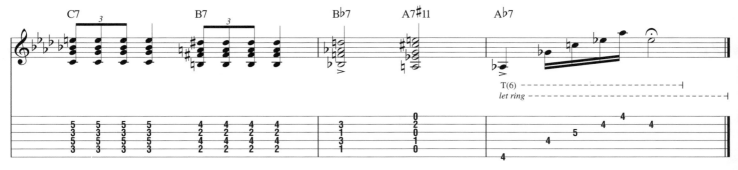

The World Is Waiting for the Sunrise

Words by Eugene Lockhart
Music by Ernest Seitz

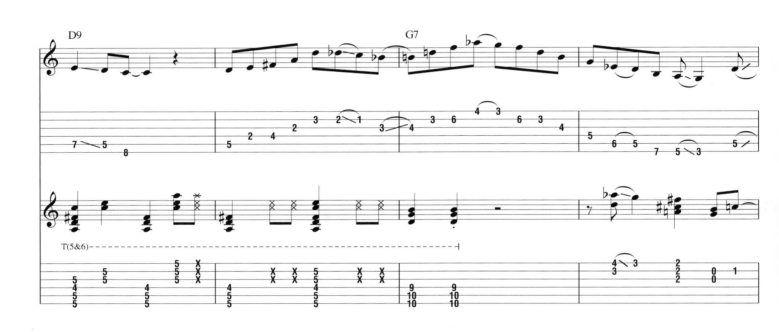

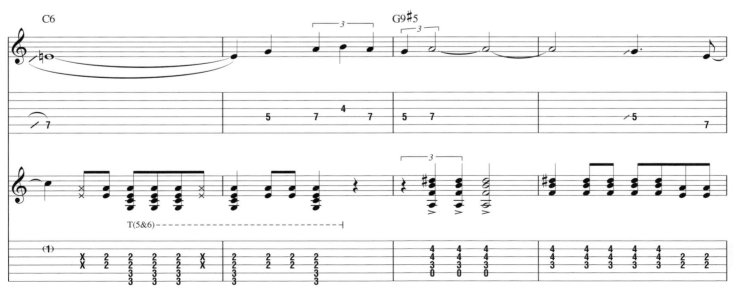

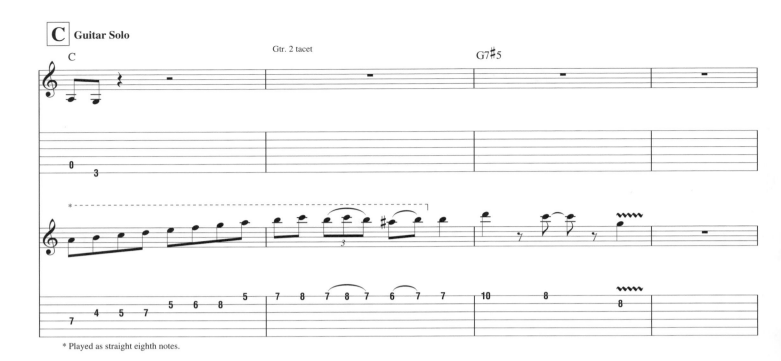

* Played as straight eighth notes.

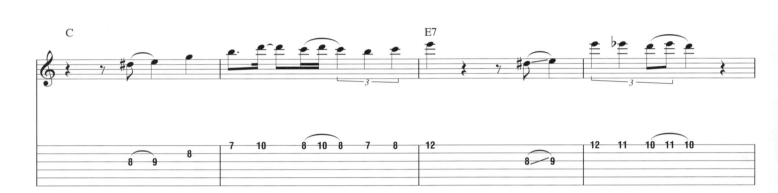

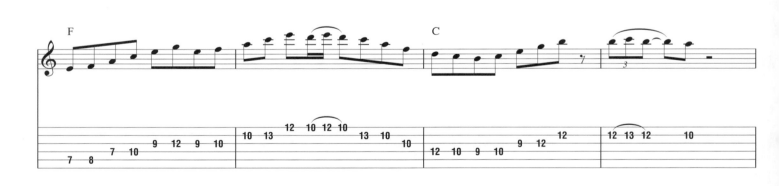

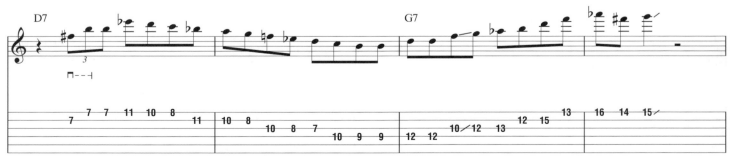

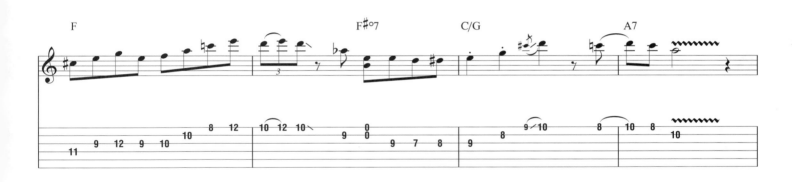

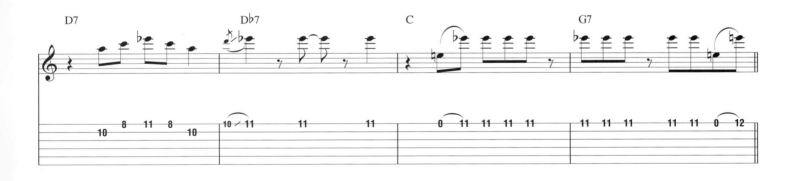

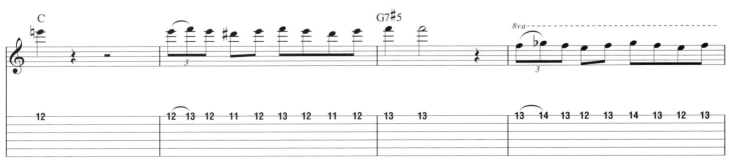

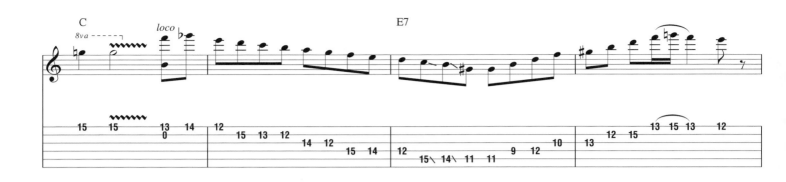

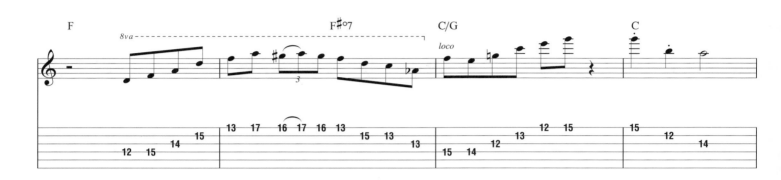

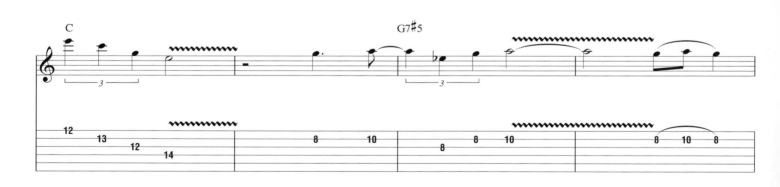

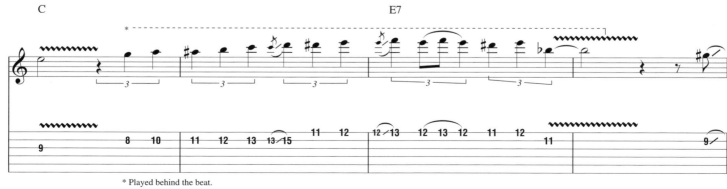

* Played behind the beat.

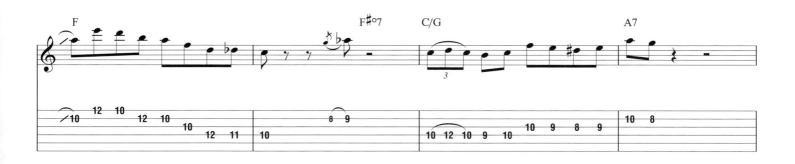

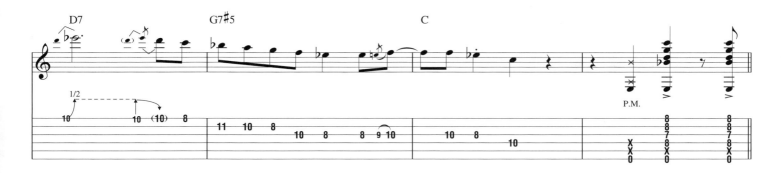

D **Piano Solo**

Gtr. 1 tacet

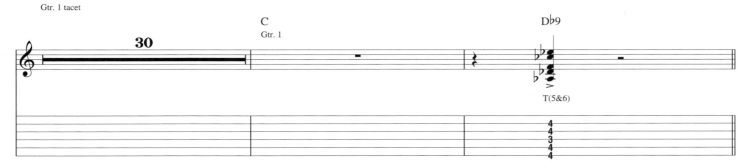

E **Violin Solo**

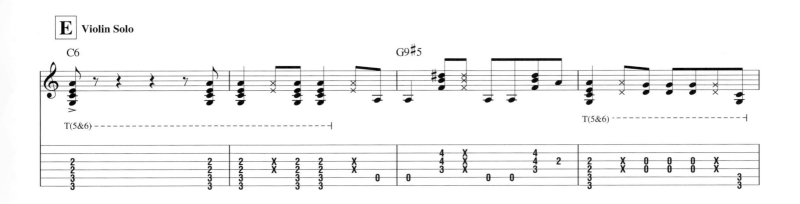

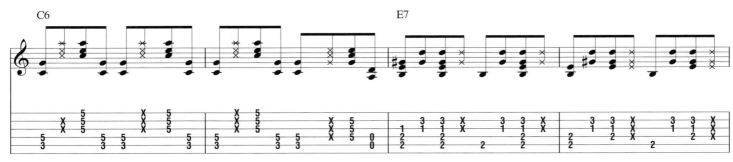

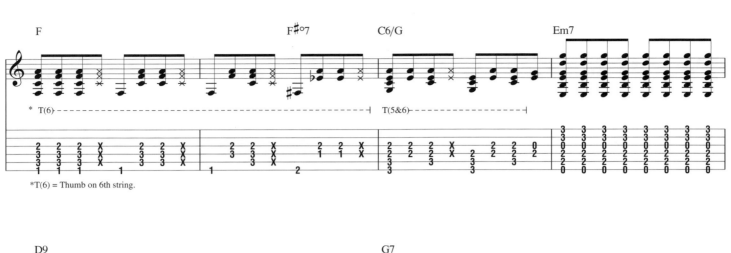

*T(6) = Thumb on 6th string.

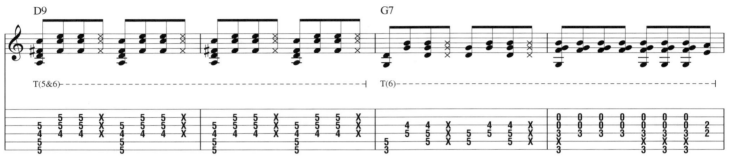

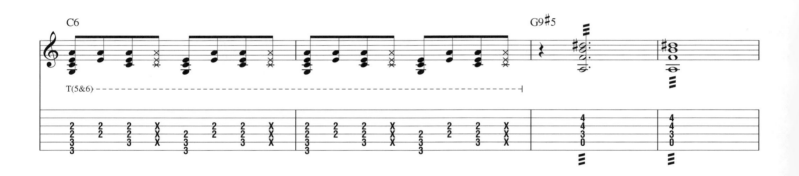

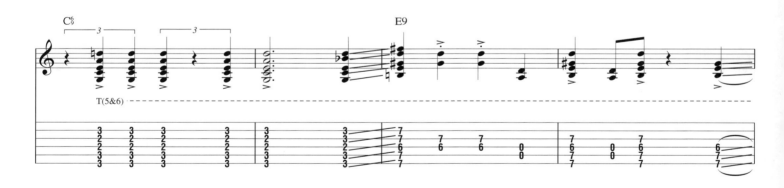

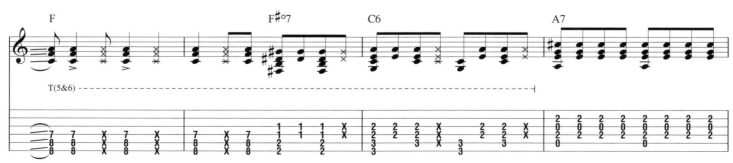

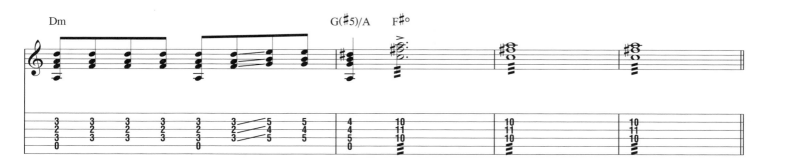

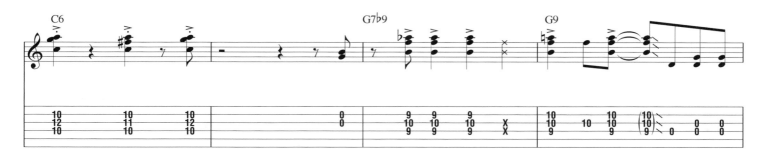

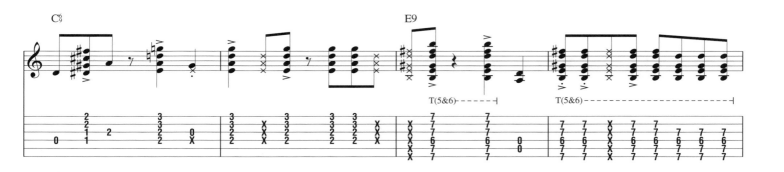

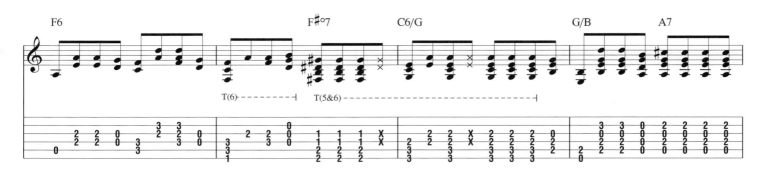

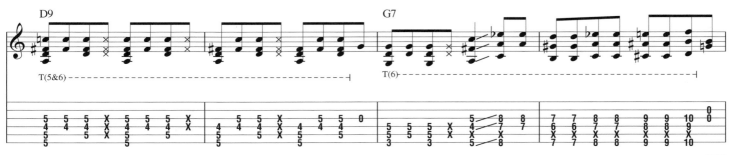

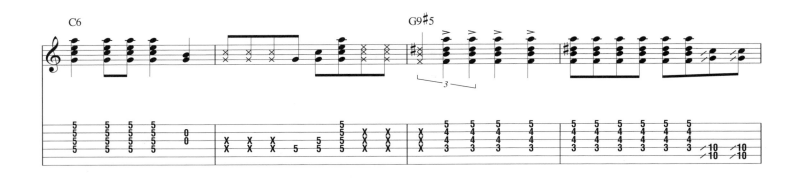

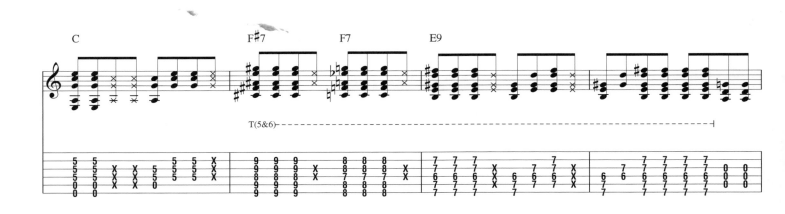

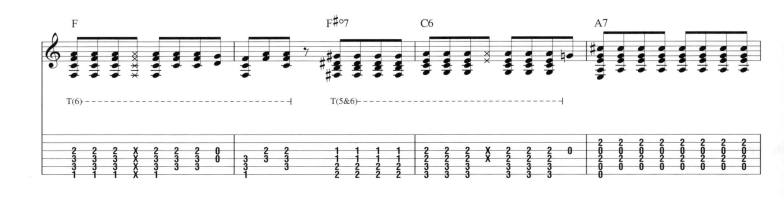

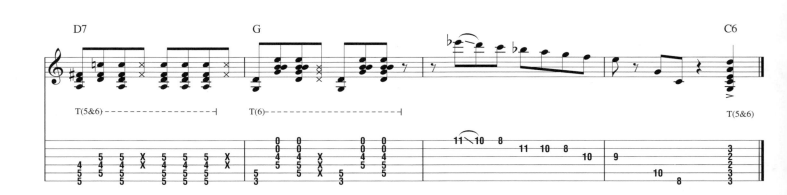

Guitar Notation Legend

Guitar Music can be notated three different ways: on a *musical staff*, in *tablature*, and in *rhythm slashes*.

RHYTHM SLASHES are written above the staff. Strum chords in the rhythm indicated. Use the chord diagrams found at the top of the first page of the transcription for the appropriate chord voicings. Round noteheads indicate single notes.

THE MUSICAL STAFF shows pitches and rhythms and is divided by bar lines into measures. Pitches are named after the first seven letters of the alphabet.

TABLATURE graphically represents the guitar fingerboard. Each horizontal line represents a string, and each number represents a fret.

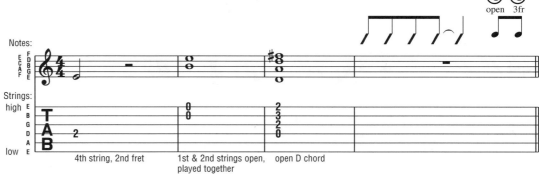

4th string, 2nd fret   1st & 2nd strings open, played together   open D chord

HALF-STEP BEND: Strike the note and bend up 1/2 step.

WHOLE-STEP BEND: Strike the note and bend up one step.

GRACE NOTE BEND: Strike the note and immediately bend up as indicated.

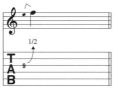

SLIGHT (MICROTONE) BEND: Strike the note and bend up 1/4 step.

BEND AND RELEASE: Strike the note and bend up as indicated, then release back to the original note. Only the first note is struck.

PRE-BEND: Bend the note as indicated, then strike it.

VIBRATO: The string is vibrated by rapidly bending and releasing the note with the fretting hand.

WIDE VIBRATO: The pitch is varied to a greater degree by vibrating with the fretting hand.

HAMMER-ON: Strike the first (lower) note with one finger, then sound the higher note (on the same string) with another finger by fretting it without picking.

PULL-OFF: Place both fingers on the notes to be sounded. Strike the first note and without picking, pull the finger off to sound the second (lower) note.

LEGATO SLIDE: Strike the first note and then slide the same fret-hand finger up or down to the second note. The second note is not struck.

SHIFT SLIDE: Same as legato slide, except the second note is struck.

TRILL: Very rapidly alternate between the notes indicated by continuously hammering on and pulling off.

TAPPING: Hammer ("tap") the fret indicated with the pick-hand index or middle finger and pull off to the note fretted by the fret hand.

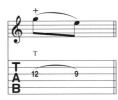

NATURAL HARMONIC: Strike the note while the fret-hand lightly touches the string directly over the fret indicated.

PINCH HARMONIC: The note is fretted normally and a harmonic is produced by adding the edge of the thumb or the tip of the index finger of the pick hand to the normal pick attack.

PICK SCRAPE: The edge of the pick is rubbed down (or up) the string, producing a scratchy sound.

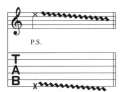

MUFFLED STRINGS: A percussive sound is produced by laying the fret hand across the string(s) without depressing, and striking them with the pick hand.

PALM MUTING: The note is partially muted by the pick hand lightly touching the string(s) just before the bridge.

RAKE: Drag the pick across the strings indicated with a single motion.

TREMOLO PICKING: The note is picked as rapidly and continuously as possible.

VIBRATO BAR DIVE AND RETURN: The pitch of the note or chord is dropped a specified number of steps (in rhythm) then returned to the original pitch.

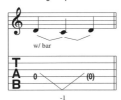

VIBRATO BAR SCOOP: Depress the bar just before striking the note, then quickly release the bar.

VIBRATO BAR DIP: Strike the note and then immediately drop a specified number of steps, then release back to the original pitch.

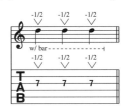

175